ENDORSEMENTS

Looking for a refreshing reminder of your place in God's kingdom? Then this is the book for you! In *God Glimpses from the Jewelry Box: Becoming Jewels God Can Use,* Michelle Cox and John Perrodin wrap spiritual truth around ordinary items found in jewelry boxes. Beckoning titles such as "Broken Jewelry," "A Pet Collar," "Diamonds," and "The Charm Bracelet" invite readers to ponder their own treasured status. In addition to poignant stories, each of the thirty chapters contains an encouraging quotation, prayer, and Scripture—and ends with the thought-provoking "Jewelry Insurance Inventory Form."

—SANDRA P. ALDRICH, author
of *Heart Hugs for Single Moms: 52 Devotions to Encourage You*

God Glimpses from the Jewelry Box is a lovely collection of devotions designed to help readers find the jewels hidden in everyday life. I especially like the "Jewelry Insurance Inventory Form" at the end of each chapter that asks readers to consider where *their* treasure is and encourages them to store up treasures in heaven—those that will never lose their value. A jewel of a book!

—DEBORAH RANEY, author of *Because of the Rain*
and the Chicory Inn novels

In the time it takes to choose and put on your jewelry, Michelle Cox and John Perrodin will inspire and encourage your walk with God. In *God Glimpses from the Jewelry Box: Becoming Jewels God Can Use,* you will gain gems from God's Word that will enlighten and energize each and every day to create a priceless future.

—PAM AND BILL FARREL, authors of forty-five books,
including *7 Simple Skills for Every Woman*
and *7 Simple Skills for Every Man*

Catching a glimpse of God is one of the great joys and encouragements in our daily walk with the Lord. I'm so glad Michelle and John wrote the *God Glimpses* books. It's a brilliant concept—stuffing jewelry boxes and toolboxes with clever concepts to enhance our relationship with God.

—TODD STARNES, *Fox News* channel

You can't do better than my friends Michelle Cox and John Perrodin if you're looking for spiritual guidance leading to real growth. When I think of them both, what comes to mind beyond their commitment to stellar writing and careful scriptural scholarship is a deep love for God and a reverence for His Word. Add to that their examples as spouses and parents in two long-term marriages, and you have a pair of authors uniquely qualified to mine the unsearchable riches of Christ. Immerse yourself in *God Glimpses* ... and come away more disciplined, consistent, and prepared to serve.

—JERRY B. JENKINS, novelist and biographer, JerryJenkins.com

If there is one thing I hold dear in my heart, it's the heirloom jewelry in my jewelry box ... not necessarily for the monetary value, but because of the stories my mother shared with me as she showed them to me, back when they took up residence in the velvety recesses of her own jewelry box. But even more important than the jewelry passed down from great-great-grandmothers, great-aunts, grandmothers, and my own mother is the legacy of being a woman after God's heart, which they also passed on to me. Within the words of this book, Michelle Cox has brilliantly woven the joy of the bling with the truth of the jewels, and the high value of God glimpses from the jewelry box.

—EVA MARIE EVERSON, best-selling author, *Five Brides*

My friend, author Michelle Cox, who wears "bling for the King," has written a sparkling new devotional, *God Glimpses from the Jewelry Box*, that will perfectly fit anyone who loves to shine! Dig in and discover the treasures that are sometimes hidden under tarnished heirloom silver or the tossed aside strand of priceless pearls. Though you wear your charm bracelet every day, did you ever think of each charm as a memento of God's faithfulness? Cox takes us through thirty different kinds of jewelry, inserting fascinating stories and prompting us to ask questions of our heart and soul in the process. Who knew that a pocket watch and earrings could spur us on to greater commitment to God who is the Creator of all true jewels? I greatly enjoyed this devotional and highly recommend it for those like me who fill half our luggage with statement necklaces!

—LUCINDA SECREST MCDOWELL, author of *Dwelling Places*, EncouragingWords.net

From the time I was a tiny girl, I had a fascination with jewelry. I spent hours going through both my mother's and my grandmother's jewelry boxes—each piece telling a story. Michelle and John have captured just that, the reminiscent feeling of pouring through those boxes. I will not be able to look at my own jewelry box the same. Instead of the glitz and bling, I now see the fingerprints of God and my life story. This book will be my go-to gift for all my girlfriends. This is a "curl up on the couch with a cup of coffee" feel-good book. Now I'm going to accessorize, accessorize, and sparkle for Jesus!

—CAROL HATCHER, sassy, Southern, sparkly boot-wearing wife and mother of three; writer and international speaker

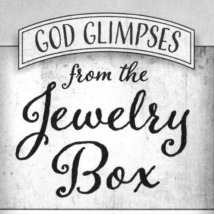

GOD GLIMPSES

from the Jewelry Box

BECOMING JEWELS GOD CAN USE

MICHELLE COX
AND JOHN PERRODIN

BroadStreet
PUBLISHING

BroadStreet Publishing Group, LLC
Racine, Wisconsin, USA
BroadStreetPublishing.com

God Glimpses from the Jewelry Box
BECOMING JEWELS GOD CAN USE

ISBN-13: 978-1-4245-5209-2 (hardcover)
ISBN-13: 978-1-4245-5210-8 (e-book)

Quotes from the authors are so identified. Quotes in chapters 2–3, 6–7, 9–10, 15, 17–18, 20, 23, 26–27, and 29 are taken from Worth Repeating © 2003 by Bob Kelly. Published by Kregel Publications, Grand Rapids, MI. Used by permission of the publisher. All rights reserved. All other quotes are in the public domain and sourced with appreciation to www.bartelby.com.

Scripture quotations are taken from the King James Version of the Bible and sourced with appreciation to www.biblegateway.com.

Stock or custom editions of BroadStreet Publishing titles may be purchased in bulk for educational, business, ministry, fundraising, or sales promotional use. For information, please e-mail info@broadstreetpublishing.com.

Cover design by Chris Garborg, garborgdesign.com
Interior design and typesetting by Katherine Lloyd, TheDESKonline.com

Printed in China

16 17 18 19 20 5 4 3 2 1

And they shall be mine, saith the LORD of hosts,
in that day when I make up my jewels.

—*Malachi 3:17*

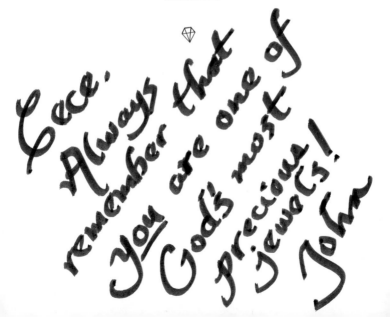

Cece,
Always that
remember
You are one of
God's most
precious
jewels!
John

Contents

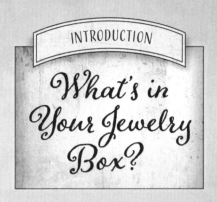

INTRODUCTION

What's in Your Jewelry Box?

Girlfriends, what's in your jewelry boxes? I (Michelle) asked that question recently on Facebook, and the results were fascinating. I was surprised by how many responses I received. Yes, women keep jewelry in their jewelry boxes, but they also store a wide variety of other things in those treasure chests—everything from baby teeth and safety pins to love letters and military medals.

God Glimpses from the Jewelry Box: Becoming Jewels God Can Use is the first release in the God Glimpses book series. God often mentions jewels in the Bible. And that's awesome since most of us girls love our sparkly accessories.

When we look into our jewelry boxes, it's easy to see the items we keep in there. But what most of us haven't discovered before are the amazing spiritual lessons hiding in our jewelry boxes.

We sometimes act as if God is a million miles away when just the opposite is true. Glimpses of God are present in every aspect of our lives if we'll open our eyes and look around. That's the premise for the *God Glimpses* books: to take important spiritual truths and apply them to ordinary things such as a building project, a visit to the spa, a day at the office, or the items found in a jewelry box or toolbox. We *can* discover God's will and purpose for our lives if we'll just take time to catch a glimpse of Him.

God Glimpses from the Jewelry Box features thirty things found in a woman's jewelry box. Each of the chapters includes a definition of the item and a story with a spiritual application. We've also added a quote, a prayer, and a verse of Scripture to help us on our quest to become priceless jewels in God's jewelry box. A "Jewelry Insurance Inventory Form" at the end of each chapter provides thought-provoking questions suitable for quiet times, family devotions, small groups, or an evening with girlfriends. And all of them will lead to one important question for each of us to consider: What's your treasure?

Sweet friends, I don't know about you, but I want to be bling for the King. I want to shine and sparkle for Him. Will you join me as we look for God glimpses from the jewelry box?

ONE

Silver Jewelry

Silver is a precious metal. It's lightly colored and can be polished to a bright shine. Silver must be cleaned regularly to keep it from tarnishing. It is easily fashioned into new forms and must go through a refining process to remove unwanted materials. Since pure silver is often too soft, sterling silver (which is silver that has been mixed with a small amount of other metals) is usually used for jewelry. Silver jewelry blends well with a variety of fashions and can be worn for any occasion.

A tarnished life can shine again
when polished with God's love.

—Michelle Cox

SYLVIA WAS THRILLED TO INHERIT her grandmother's jewelry box. It was filled with memories of wonderful days that she and Grandma Bessie had spent together. Picking up a silver brooch, she rubbed the tarnish, trying to wipe it away.

While playing in her mother's jewelry box as a little girl, Sylvia had broken so much jewelry that she wasn't allowed to play in it anymore. But Grandma Bessie couldn't resist those big blue eyes, so Sylvia was given free rein with her grandmother's jewelry box.

Even better, Sylvia's grandmother played *with* her, both of them in elegant attire, draped with strand after strand of pearls and beads. Sylvia teared up as those memories flooded back.

She hadn't realized it as a child, but such love had been evident in those moments ... in the brownies they'd baked for their tea parties ... in the time her grandmother had so freely given ... and in the laughter and conversation they'd shared.

As Sylvia became a teen, those jewelry box moments changed. They were still special, just different. She'd spent sunny afternoons sprawled on the porch with Grandma Bessie, sharing the history behind each item.

The silver brooch had been her grandmother's most prized piece of jewelry. It was the last gift from Sylvia's grandfather. Grandma Bessie received it a week after she'd learned the news of his death while fighting in World War II.

And, now, they were both gone. Sylvia ran her finger

across the brooch, remembering the day her grandmother had shared the story about it. She could almost hear her sweet voice.

"Sylvia, this is special to me for a number of reasons. Obviously, because it's the last gift from Granddaddy James, but even more because this silver brooch sums up what your granddaddy's life was all about." Her voice had cracked as she'd continued, "Granddaddy always bought me silver jewelry because he said it reminded him of serving Jesus. I remember the day he gave me a ring. He told me, 'Bessie, to make silver pure, it has to go through a refining process. The metal must be screened to remove unwanted materials from the silver. And then it's heated again and again until it's pure. It's like our spiritual lives. The wisdom of the years spent in His Word can make us shine. Or we can come out gritty and tarnished because we haven't taken the time to care for our souls. Let's shine for Him, sweetheart.'"

As Sylvia placed the brooch back into the jewelry box, she whispered, "God, I'm sorry I forgot about you. I think it's time to remove the tarnish from the brooch ... and my life. Thank you for grandparents who left me an inheritance of faith."

What kind of inheritance are *you* leaving behind?

◇ ◇

For thou, O God, hast proved us:
thou hast tried us, as silver is tried.

—*Psalm 66:10*

Dear God, I don't want my life and my testimony to be tarnished. Refine me. Remove the impurities. Form me into what you want for my life. Help my heart to be soft like silver so that I'm pliable for your use. Help me to shine for you in a world that needs to see your light. Thank you for those who have invested in me. And when someone sees a bit of discoloration hampering my testimony, give them the strength to tell me—and give me the courage to hear the truth. Amen.

THE JEWELRY INSURANCE INVENTORY FORM

What is your treasure?

1. Have you ever wondered why you face trials? Pray and ask God to show you what He wants you to learn from those moments.

2. The silver brooch was tarnished because it hadn't received proper care. Is there tarnish in your life? Is there an area that you need to address?

3. Grandma Bessie's time was a precious gift to her granddaughter. Do you spend enough time with your family? Are you spending your days in God's Word ... or in technology?

4. Just as Sylvia's grandmother shared her stories, have you shared your stories of faith with your family? Did your grandfather leave behind favorite passages of Scripture? Was there a church or an individual who impacted your life spiritually? Have you told your children about your salvation experience? Pass those stories down to another generation.

TWO

Broken Jewelry

Broken jewelry is jewelry that has been damaged, has lost a clasp or a fastener, or is missing a matching piece, a stone, or a bead. Some people prefer to toss such worthless items. They have neither the time nor skill to fix them. Often the broken jewelry seems like it's too far gone to keep, but sometimes a little glue, some paint, or a replacement piece can make it usable again. In the right hands, a trinket of little value can be restored to its former beauty and shine, just as God has done for many of us.

Man is born broken. He lives by mending.
And the grace of God is glue.

—Eugene O'Neill

FROM BROKEN TO USEFUL

For someone who can't stand clutter, I sure seem to collect a lot of it. Even in my jewelry box. One day when I have some extra time, I need to go through it and get rid of all the junk that's in there.

Oh, c'mon, you know you have some too. At least, I don't *think* I'm the only jewelry hoarder on the planet. I've got broken pieces of jewelry in my jewelry box. Yes, broken pieces. A little glue, a dab of paint, a new clasp, and they'll be as good as new—if I ever get around to fixing them.

There are necklaces with loose links. When I wear them, the necklace falls off because the links come apart. You'd think I'd have learned the first time it happened, but I seem to be a slow learner in that regard. All I need to do is to take a tool and tighten the links—and I'll do that ... eventually.

There are single earrings. I can't find their mates, but I can't throw them away because I might find the other one someday. Crazy, huh? I mean, it's never happened in my lifetime, but a girl can hope, can't she? I also have earrings with missing backs. I keep meaning to buy a pack of replacement fasteners, but I'll do that someday if I think of it while I'm out shopping.

There are rings with missing stones. I can have a new stone put in, so I can't throw them away. I actually have accomplished this once—but it took me several years to get around to it.

Does any of the above sound familiar? When it comes

right down to it, that broken jewelry is basically junk because it can't be worn and enjoyed as it's supposed to be.

You know what, friends? We're much like that broken jewelry. When God looks into His jewelry box of souls, He sees shining jewels, but He also sees broken hearts and messed-up lives.

He sees women who are damaged by circumstances. Maybe it was the loss of someone we loved, or an unexpected diagnosis at the doctor's office. Or maybe it was from financial devastation or a prodigal child who broke our hearts. Sometimes it's even our own fault for making wrong choices. Whatever the cause, those circumstances have left damage behind, damage that keeps us from being all that He desires us to be.

I'm so grateful God doesn't throw us away when we're broken, and He's never too busy to restore us to shining usefulness for Him.

I don't want to be a broken piece in His box of treasures. I want to shine and be useful for all that He has planned for my life. How about you?

He healeth the broken in heart,
and bindeth up their wounds.
—*Psalm 147:3*

Father, so much about my life has been broken. Big things, little things, obvious things, secret things. You could have thrown me away without a second thought, yet you loved me in spite of my brokenness. You looked beyond the damaged pieces of my life and saw something of value. That you never give up on me simply overwhelms me! Thank you for your grace and mercy. Thank you for lovingly fixing the broken things in my life so I can be more useful for you. Give me compassionate vision for those in my life who are also facing brokenness. Show me ways to bring them to you—the master jewelry repairman. Amen.

THE JEWELRY INSURANCE INVENTORY FORM

What is your treasure?

1. Just as we have our broken jewelry, we have damaged things in our lives. What area of your life is broken? How has that affected you?

2. A broken heart can touch us in many ways. Has it impacted your health? Has it affected your spiritual life or relationships?

3. We hang onto broken jewelry, and sometimes we hang onto things in our lives that we need to let go of. Do you need to release worry, fear, or some sin in your life? Have you prayed about it? Are there steps you need to take?

4. God could have thrown us away, but instead He loved us enough to fix the broken areas of our lives. Make a list of what God has done for you—and then spend some time thanking Him.

THREE

The Charm Bracelet

A charm bracelet is a chain-link bracelet with decorative tokens or charms hanging from it. The collection of charms can provide a fascinating history of where we've been and what we have experienced. Each small memento has a cherished place in our hearts. That's the idea, really—to collect memories. Our bracelets become a series of miniature snapshots. Each memory, each moment, has a special place in each charm. And as we experience more, we add memorable charms as a way to celebrate.

When we look back at the faithfulness of God,
we praise Him. When we look forward
to God's faithfulness, we trust Him.

—Ken Watters

Great Is Thy Faithfulness

The simple charm bracelet is one of the most prized possessions in the jewelry box because it gives tangible reasons to remember the past and believe in the future. The charms with each of our children's or grandchildren's names make us pause and give thanks. Another charm representing our beloved dog or cared-for feline makes us think of how much a part of the family that furry four-legged friend has been. Other charms list a name or a small token of family vacations or romantic moments with our sweethearts.

They are tiny touchstones that pull us back to reality. And sometimes they can also serve as reminders that God has been there *for* us and *with* us in every circumstance.

The human memory is a curious thing. Although we know that God's faithfulness shimmers and shines throughout our lives, sometimes we find our doubts growing. When we don't receive expected answers to prayer, we wonder what has happened to us that we no longer receive the answers we once did. It's a sign and symptom of the world we live in, a world in which others (and sometimes even God) are valued only for their latest achievement.

Yesterday's accomplishments are often washed away in the constant pressure to keep producing. Even children can sometimes learn to think they aren't valued unless they're pleasing their parents. And children may look upon their parents as a credit card with no debt limit. What's missing from many of our lives is an honest reflection of how good our God is, day in and day out.

And that's where our charm bracelets can draw us toward the truth. The truth that we are loved, that we have a place in a family, that we have experienced countless blessings. Just as the wandering Israelites swiftly forgot the miracles of God, we sometimes do the same.

We forget how He protected us during a difficult delivery at the birth center. Or how a grandchild accepted Christ at a young age. Or how a stranger helped us on the road during a long road trip. Each charm is a bright spot in our life. A bejeweled marker along life's twisty-turny journey.

Let's take the time to count our charms—and our blessings—the next time we slip those bracelets on our wrists. Let's think about what's happening in our lives now and consider adding to our very personal collections.

Do we need some praying hands? A reminder to seek our lost joy? A shout of thanks to our heavenly Father for a dose of encouragement from an unusual source? These days we can find practically any charm we want. Let's seek God first and His kingdom, but keep fingering those charming tokens so that we can reflect on His faithfulness and give praise in all things.

◆ ◆

It is of the LORD's mercies that we are not consumed,
because his compassions fail not.
They are new every morning:
great is thy faithfulness.
—*Lamentations 3:22–23*

Oh Lord, the days pass quickly and I often miss jotting down anecdotes of my children, grandchildren, friends, and loved ones. Help me to celebrate the seasons with them and to be mindful of the gifts you've given me. Just as when I look at my charm bracelet and see special moments in my life, I can look back and see your faithfulness throughout each day. Thank you, precious Lord, for giving me a life that is so full and for the hidden joys even amidst the unexpected sorrows. Help me to reflect on your bounty and your love each day, for your mercy and your good gifts overwhelm me. Amen.

◆ ◆

THE JEWELRY INSURANCE INVENTORY FORM

What is your treasure?

1. What are some of the most memorable touchstones of your life? What are some of the most memorable moments of God's faithfulness in your life?

2. God is a faithful God, but we often fall short of being faithful to Him. How do you think that affects Him? Find three verses about being faithful. Pray and ask God to help you become one of His most faithful servants.

3. What are some examples of times when things didn't turn out as you'd expected? What did you learn from those situations?

4. Our charm bracelets provide reminders of where we've been. In the same manner, we can look back at our lives and see countless blessings. List some of the blessings God has granted to you and your family—and then praise Him.

FOUR

Diamonds

Diamonds are valuable and highly coveted gems that are mined from the earth. They are one of the hardest substances found in nature, which gives them great durability when used in pieces of jewelry. One reason that diamonds are considered so precious is because they are scarce and it's often difficult to obtain them. Diamonds are the most popular choice for engagement rings, and they typically come at a very high price, but most folks would agree that it's worth it in both sentimental and actual value.

Forget the diamonds—
Jesus is a girl's best friend.

—*Michelle Cox*

ONE OF GOD'S DIAMONDS

The movie star glided down the red carpet at the film premiere. Her designer gown was gorgeous, but most noticeable were all the diamonds that sparkled around her neck. They also dangled from her ears and enlaced her wrists. She stopped in front of the banner and posed for photos, turning slowly so that the photographers could catch her at different angles. That was a wise move because with all that bling, she'd have looked like a disco ball if she'd turned any faster.

When the members of the media asked her about her glittering accessories, the star replied, "They're worth more than a million dollars." She named the jewelry store that had loaned them to her and then said, "That's why I have a security guard as my date for the evening."

Besides being one of the most valuable items in our jewelry boxes, diamonds have some awesome traits. They are mined from the earth, and they're one of the hardest, most durable substances found in nature. When purchasing a diamond, we're supposed to watch for the four Cs—color, cut, clarity, and carats. Since they are so costly, one might think that diamonds would be perfect, but if you use a loupe (the magnifying glass used by most jewelers) and take a close look, there are imperfections.

Every prospective groom desires to buy his bride-to-be a quality diamond. He doesn't want one with a murky color or one that isn't cut well. He knows the love of his life will enjoy watching her ring twinkle as she proudly twists her hand in the sunshine.

He'll also discover quickly that the more carats there are in his fiancée's ring, the more money he will shell out, but because he loves her so much, he's willing to pay the price.

You know, our spiritual lives are much like that of the movie star who was draped in diamonds. Everything we have is on loan from God. Just as diamonds are mined from the earth, God reached down into the dirt and dust of our sin, making us into His jewels. We're *valuable* to Him.

I want to be one of God's diamonds, durable until I've completed the plan He has for me. I want my heart to sparkle for Him—and I want to reflect His love to others.

Just as that young sweetheart paid the price for a diamond for his bride, God paid the price for us—and He did it willingly because He loves us. And the really awesome thing? When God looks at us through His loupe of grace, He knows the imperfections that are there—and He still makes it possible for us to sparkle for Him.

Let your light so shine before men,
that they may see your good works,
and glorify your Father which is in heaven.

—*Matthew 5:16*

I want to be sold-out for you, Father, durable and strong for the journey of life. It boggles my mind to realize you look at me and see something of value. I want to fulfill the plan you have for me. Just as that movie star's diamonds sparkled on the red carpet, I want my heart to sparkle for you, and I want to reflect you and your love to a world that needs to know about you. Make me a diamond for you. Give me strength, courage, and the ability to withstand difficulties. And after all is said and done, make me shine for you. Amen.

THE JEWELRY INSURANCE INVENTORY FORM

What is your treasure?

1. The movie star's diamonds were on display on the red carpet. What is on display in our lives? Is everything all about us or is it all about Jesus? What adjustments do we need to make?

2. Diamonds are one of the strongest substances in nature. How do we compare as Christians? Do we stand strong when faced with temptations, or are we weak?

3. What do you think will make you stronger and more durable spiritually? What steps do you need to take to accomplish that? Take a few minutes to pray. Ask God to make you a strong and mighty Christian.

4. Has it really registered that God looks at you and sees something valuable? Say this: "[Your name] is valuable to God." How does that affect you?

FIVE

The Family Keepsake

Family keepsakes are sometimes put in jewelry boxes for safekeeping. The funny thing about a family treasure is that there are often differences of opinion about whether an item has lasting value or just needs to be dumped in the trash. Keepsakes are often jewelry, such as a prized locket handed down from a grandmother or a pocket watch that belonged to a grandfather, but they can include other sentimental items as well. Sometimes it takes the story behind the keepsake to show the rest of the clan that it's worth hanging on to.

Sometimes we spend so much time dwelling on
our past that we forget to focus on our future.

—Michelle Cox

An Unexpected Discovery

Finding jewelry in a jewelry box is a no-brainer, but sometimes special family keepsakes can be found there as well. I have a worn leather notebook in my jewelry box that's one of my most prized possessions. Let me share the story behind that.

I was devastated when my dad passed away. Emptying his house so we could put it on the market was a mammoth task. Dad lived in another state, and we had limited time to pack his belongings, so boxes were packed into the moving truck with just a quick glance at the contents.

Months later I was still going through containers. One box I'd hauled to our den looked like it was all junk. I almost threw everything in the trash without looking through the items, but I'm glad I didn't. I would have thrown away something that's a treasure to me.

You see, buried in that box of junk was a little leather notebook. When I opened it, I found my dad's familiar handwriting, pages filled with details of his journeys as well as names and addresses of his fellow sailors from their time on a ship during World War II.

That was a precious find. The history was fascinating, but then I found the pages that made me cry. They were the ones where my daddy had marked off the days until he'd be home. Page after page of days with check marks beside them.

I have many photos of my dad in his US Navy uniform. The day I found the notebook, I could almost see Dad as a homesick young sailor sitting on his bunk, missing his family and friends, checking off another day that would bring him that much closer to being home with them again. It was clear that despite the horrible experiences he went through during those times of war, Dad's focus was on making it home.

You know, friends, sometimes we become so focused on the here and now that we forget there's a far more important eternity waiting for us. That's something for all of us to think about.

The first consideration is to have assurance that we're ready to meet God—that we've surrendered our lives, asked forgiveness for our sins, and asked Jesus into our hearts.

And the second consideration? What if we lived our lives in a manner where we were counting the days until we got to be with Jesus? None of us knows how long we have before that day will arrive. For some it might be years away, and for others, it might be soon.

Just as my daddy was faithful to record everyday events in that little notebook that's tucked in my jewelry box, let's keep our focus on doing the job God has for us to do until we get home—and on making it there with our mission accomplished.

But none of these things move me,
neither count I my life dear unto myself, so that
I might finish my course with joy, and the ministry, which
I have received of the Lord Jesus,
to testify the gospel of the grace of God.

—*Acts 20:24*

I'm so grateful I'm part of your family, Father. Thank you for the gift of salvation that makes me your child. As I go about my day, remind me to be intentional about living for you. When the battles come in my life, help me to be faithful. Help me to serve you with joy, and as the days count down until I'll meet you in heaven, help me to finish the course you've set before me and to fulfill the mission and ministry you have for me to do. Amen.

THE JEWELRY INSURANCE INVENTORY FORM

What is your treasure?

1. The discovery of my dad's little notebook was unexpected, but it so touched my heart. What's your favorite unexpected discovery in God's Word, and how did that impact you?

2. My dad was far from home, missing those he loved. All of us experience that lonely feeling from time to time. How has God showed up to be with you during those moments?

3. God has a purpose for each of our lives—a mission and a ministry. If we don't fulfill His plan for us, then it will remain undone or He'll give that blessing to someone else. Has He nudged your heart to do something for Him? What are you doing about that?

4. Are you ready to meet Jesus? Is everything well with your soul? If not, now would be a good time to take care of that.

SIX

A Strand of Pearls

Pearls are often given as a special gift to commemorate a momentous occasion, such as a bride's wedding day. A strand of pearls is a necklace that's been strung on a silk cord, and it's usually finished off with a decorative clasp. The jeweler makes a knot between each pearl and then gives it a slight pull to tighten the knot. The knotting provides security to prevent multiple pearls from being lost in case of breakage. It also protects the pearls from rubbing against each other, which can result in marring and chipping.

God loves each of us
as if there were only one of us.

—*St. Augustine*

Pearls of Great Value

"Wait a minute, Melissa," Amy said. "Let's look through that box again before you throw it out. Do you think that strand of pearls might be valuable?"

Melissa looked skeptically at her friend. "I don't think real pearls would be stuck in a box of cheap toys."

Melissa's mom had passed away a few weeks earlier, and the two friends were emptying her house for the new tenants. Since Melissa's mom had been a hoarder, it was quite a task. Some of the rooms were inaccessible since they were piled to the ceiling with boxes. Others only had a tiny path through them to a couch or bed. Even the bathtub and oven were crammed with things.

Melissa and Amy had spent weeks going through the piles. It looked like they hadn't even made a dent. They'd filled a moving van to capacity and packed the car full numerous times. Melissa had given items to family members, multiple loads had gone to Goodwill, and they'd thrown out more than two hundred bags of trash. Yet the house still looked almost as it had when they started. Long weeks of sorting and packing still stretched ahead of them. So you can understand Melissa's doubt that the pearls in the box of toys might be real. But she listened when Amy said, "Why don't we have a jeweler look at them before we throw them away?"

"Okay, but don't be disappointed when he laughs and says they're worthless."

A few weeks later, the friends met with a jewelry appraiser.

"Sir, we found some pearls in a box of junk toys that belonged to my mother," Melissa said. "I think they're worthless, but my friend thinks they might have some value. Would you look at them and see what you think?"

The jeweler removed the pearls from the bag. He clasped his hands around the cold strand of pearls, feeling them warm from the heat of his hands. Then he cleaned them with gentle care. "Oh my," he said softly as he took a close look. "Girls, not only are these pearls real, they're extremely valuable. The luster is amazing and the hand knotting is superb. These are some of the finest quality pearls I've ever seen."

Just as Melissa looked at the strand of pearls and thought they were junk, I wonder how many times each of us have looked at ourselves and thought, *I'm worthless.*

That's when God looks at us and says, *Wait a minute. You might not think you're worth much, but I see something of immense value. I paid a great price for you, and you're priceless to me.*

Then He clasps His loving hands around us, spreading His warmth into our lives. He cleans away the imperfections and then says, *Worthless? Not a chance!* Because in His eyes, we're one of His precious jewels.

Again, the kingdom of heaven is like
unto a merchant man, seeking goodly pearls:
Who, when he had found one pearl of great price,
went and sold all that he had, and bought it.

—Matthew 13:45–46

*Lord, thank you for paying the ultimate price for me.
I'm grateful you saw something of value in me, even
when I don't feel like I'm worth much. Thanks for
never giving up on me. Please give me your eyes to
see what others have to offer, and help me to nurture
and grow those possibilities through encouragement
and by speaking the right word at the right time.
Help me to live my life so that others will see you
when they look at me. Keep me ever bound to you
with strong strands of faith. Make me a jewel shining
brightly with your hope. Amen.*

THE JEWELRY INSURANCE INVENTORY FORM

What is your treasure?

1. Just as the jeweler cleaned the pearls, what does God need to clean in your life so that others will see the luster of a shining Christian life?

2. Melissa and Amy went through piles of junk to find the pearls. Look back at your life and make a list of things God's brought you through.

3. Melissa thought the pearls were worthless, but the jeweler saw great value in them. Sometimes we're our own worst enemies, cutting ourselves down and focusing on our flaws. What if we saw ourselves through God's eyes? What if we saw others through God's eyes? How would that change how we live each day?

4. Do you have friends who need to hear they're valuable to God? Ask God to place three people on your heart and then share that message with them.

SEVEN

A Pet Collar

A pet collar is a nylon or leather band that goes around an animal's neck. It hangs loosely and opens quickly with a buckle. A lead or leash can be attached to keep the pet safe and away from danger, including busy roads or more aggressive animals. The collar also indicates a certain relationship in which the guardian promises to care for the cat, dog, bunny, or iguana. An ID tag with your phone number may hang from the collar so if the pet is ever lost, it can be located and returned to you again.

Love sacrifices all things
to bless the thing it loves.

—*Edward G. Bulwer-Lytton*

WOMAN'S BEST FRIEND

In my mother's jewelry box, in crinkled tissue paper, is a faded pink leather band with faux gems. It's also a bit chewed. Regardless of its ratty appearance, she would never think of parting with that collar from her dear dachshund. Memories of that precious short-haired dog are priceless, especially because that stubby-legged guardian saved her life.

My mother and father had resisted the inevitable for months, but the hole left by the loss of their last pet was still gaping. They promised each other they would never again allow an animal to grab hold of their hearts so ferociously. But they couldn't resist. After a respectable time, they started visiting rescue dogs who desperately needed some TLC. That's when they found Jamocha.

Puppyish at age two, she rubbed her nose raw trying to attract visitors at the shelter. She was waiting for the right person to save her. My parents knew a keeper when they found her.

One day my mother was working in their desert yard and heard a dreaded buzzing rattle. A snake was nearby, but where? Jamocha barked, and my mother stepped back to safety. The price of Jamocha's protection was her life. The snake had struck the little dog as she went bravely ahead of her beloved mistress. Inside, the animal nursed her wounds, howling as the poison did its damage. No amount of antivenom could save her.

And so her collar holds a treasured place in the jewelry

box. No other animal will ever wear it. For it belongs only to Jamocha, a precious pet we'll never forget. God gave us such beloved animals to enrich our lives—and they do. We love and care for them, knowing deep down that we need them far more than they need us.

But the spiritual application goes even deeper, doesn't it? Think back to how the Savior collared you. What was your life like before you found His welcoming home? What did it take for you to be rescued? Many of us have long and amazing tales about coming to Christ. About how He gave His life for us, how He saved and adopted us into His big wonderful family.

And God gives us unique gifts that bolster our faith. For example, certain Scriptures have led us through low points in life, prayers from friends lifted us when we felt our faith falter, and meaningful music comforted our hearts while bringing tears to our eyes.

Besides a beloved memento of our pets, we likely will find in the jewelry box cards and notes from loved ones that helped us hang on when we thought we'd give up. Kind of like the warm lick of a furry friend or the sweet snore of a pup in your lap. Each of us needs—in whatever form—these special reminders that God truly cares.

But ask now the beasts, and they shall teach thee;
and the fowls of the air, and they shall tell thee.

—Job 12:7

Lord, you made the birds of the air, the beasts of the field, and every amazing animal on this planet. I appreciate your creativity. When we adopted our pet, I didn't know you were giving us a favorite new family member, but you did. I know at one level she's "only" a dog, but I also know how much fun that crazy critter brings me, how glad she makes my heart, and how much she delights my children and grandchildren. Thank you for being Lord of the details, great and small, and thanks for giving us opportunities to care for your creatures and to learn more about unconditional love. Amen.

THE JEWELRY INSURANCE INVENTORY FORM

What is your treasure?

1. Think about a precious memento or photo of a pet who has made a difference in the life of your family. How does God give your family the chance to help His creatures?

2. What are some ways that animals model sacrifice in the way they care for their humans? What can we learn from them? How can that apply to us spiritually?

3. When you find a small bird or rabbit that has been injured, what is your first reaction? Why do you think God wants us to stay connected to His nature?

4. Jamocha gave her life for her mistress, which was amazing, but the fact that the God of the universe gave His life for us is precious beyond words. How do you feel about that kind of love?

EIGHT

The Passport

A passport is issued by a traveler's country of origin. It allows you to leave your homeland, visit abroad, and then return again. While away from your native land, the passport becomes one of your most valuable possessions and must be carried at all times. That's because you won't be allowed to return without it. When traveling with your "pass," you still represent your own country. As a US citizen, therefore, you have certain rights no matter where you go. A passport also provides verification that you're actually the person named on the document.

God is our passport for life.
Our identity is found in Him.
—*Michelle Cox*

PASSPORT TO ADVENTURE

A passport is a wonderful tool for opening up the world in astounding ways. With this special book, you can travel to faraway foreign lands. For many travelers, the imprints made by rubber stamps when passing from country to country are irreplaceable. Every single stop comes with a story—of exotic places seen, trains missed, foods tasted, vistas viewed, and new friends met.

Each stamp represents a step in a lifelong journey. As well as visiting the official tourist sites, you likely went off on your own to concoct your own cultural adventures. Maybe you got lost for a time and had to try to communicate with muttering and mime to trace your way back to home base. Your passport is a treasured memory book that is worthy of a special and secure spot in your jewelry box.

But because that passport opens so many doors, losing it on a trip can be a supreme inconvenience. Until an emergency temporary passport is issued, you're stopped in your tracks. Instead of seeing the sights, you're stuck in line waiting. But there are good reasons for this extra care. Stolen passports can be a matter of national security, as extremists may use a valid passport to enter a country for reprehensible purposes.

A passport also opens doors to share your love for Jesus Christ with a lost and hurting world. Whether you have participated in short-term mission trips or live internationally with your family as a full-time missionary, your passport is vital to you. It tells officials in the nation you're visiting where you were born. This vital document tells what country and king you've pledged your allegiance to.

What kind of spiritual passport do you carry—and how many stamps do you have? How would a person meeting you for the very first time know that you are a believer? Does His imprint on your life show others that you're a follower of Christ?

Though almost everyone loves returning home after a journey, the fact that so many enjoy seeing new people and places shows we were not meant to stand still. God created us to keep learning and growing. Similarly, He has placed His Word in our hearts to be shared with others—not kept quietly like a secret. Mark 16:15 says, "And he said unto them, Go ye into all the world, and preach the gospel to every creature."

No matter where in the world we are, God is with us. And in all locales, we have the opportunity to speak up for our King, with or without a visible passport. We have something far better—a loyalty for life that is imprinted upon us body, mind, and soul.

◇ ◇

I will instruct thee and teach thee
in the way which thou shalt go.
—*Psalm 32:8*

Lord, make me burn to share your word. Give me a heart that weeps for those who don't know of your glory and wonders. With so many daily demands pounding at me, I sometimes forget that there are still many who need to hear the good news. I don't have to look past my own circle of friends and family to think of people who will die without knowing the truth unless someone speaks up. Show me how I can be strong and unafraid. Give me opportunities to plant seeds and nurture new believers into your heavenly kingdom.

THE JEWELRY INSURANCE INVENTORY FORM

What is your treasure?

1. Have you ever participated in a short-term mission trip or supported someone who did? How did that experience change your eternal perspective?

2. What is your own personal strategy for sharing the gospel? You may not be a preacher, but there are other ways to share Christ that can change hearts, sometimes even without speaking a word. List some options for reaching out to your friends, neighbors, and family.

3. Do you regularly pray for missionaries stationed in foreign lands? What are some other ways you could show support to them?

4. Write down reasons to rejoice that you know God personally. How are you deepening your "faith roots" so that you will continue to stand firm for Him throughout all of your life journey?

NINE

A Handmade Pin

While pins (sometimes called brooches) are often made commercially, they can also be crafted by hand. A brooch is a piece of ornamental jewelry that fastens with a clasp or pin. It can be any size or shape, reflecting the style of the owner. It's typically worn near the shoulder on a blouse, sweater, or lapel, and is sometimes used to hold the pieces of a dress or blouse together so they don't gap open. The types of pins available—and the materials used—are virtually limitless.

God's definition of beauty is a lot different
than the world's. God says that beauty
is found in a gentle, quiet, and obedient spirit.

—Heather Whitestone

FLAWED

Cindy's jewelry box is full of beautiful jewelry. She is blessed with an eye for fashion, and her pieces are both stylish and classic, each item chosen with care. Also tucked away for safekeeping in her jewelry box is a pin that most women wouldn't wear in public—especially a fashionista like Cindy.

The pin is ... well, it's a mess. The colors are tacky and the clasp is awry, making the pin hang awkwardly when she wears it. Gobs of dried glue from where a broken place was mended are clearly visible to those who examine the pin.

So why does she keep it and wear it? Cindy wears the pin because she loves the child who made it. But that's not the only reason. What Cindy's child didn't realize when she gave her mom the pin was that she was also making a spiritual object lesson for Cindy.

You see, when Cindy looks at that pin with its imperfections, it's a reflection of what God sees when He looks at her. Flaws. Mistakes. A life that has been lived poorly. Evidences of where she has pulled away from Him at various times, breaking her connection with Him. Can any of you relate? I sure can.

But that's when the master jeweler steps into our lives. With His tool kit of love and mercy, He says, *No way I'm throwing this girl away. Yes, she's flawed. Yes, she's made mistakes that have taken her away from me, but she is precious to me and I love her. She's worth whatever it takes, and before this process is over, I will fasten her so securely to me that she doesn't have to worry about falling away from me again.*

There's one other important thing about Cindy's pin that we need to realize. Even though that gift her child made for her is flawed and not as beautiful as the other pieces in Cindy's jewelry box, it can still be used for the purpose for which it was made.

That's one of the beauties of the Bible. Read through the pages, and you won't find one perfect woman there—but look how God was able to use their lives for His glory. And He can do the same with our lives, sweet friends.

You see, just like Cindy's beloved child came to her with the gift of that messed-up pin, when we come to our heavenly Father with our insufficient efforts, He sees the love that His child put into the attempt—even though the results fall short of His perfection—and His heart is touched.

I'm so grateful for a God who can take the broken pieces of our lives, glue them together with grace, and make something beautiful out of them.

He hath made every thing
beautiful in his time.
—*Ecclesiastes 3:11*

Father, I realize I am filled with imperfections and flaws, but I so want you to use my life for your glory. Help me to be pliable as you work on me. Help me to submit to your will—even when I don't understand it at the time—and to realize that you have my ultimate good in mind. Thank you for loving me. I hope that when you look at my less-than-perfect efforts, you'll see a heart that is passionately in love with you. Amen.

◆ ◆

THE JEWELRY INSURANCE INVENTORY FORM

What is your treasure?

1. God doesn't have one perfect woman in the Bible—but look at how He used their lives and how they've touched us as we've read their stories. Who is your favorite Bible woman, and what can you learn from her not-so-perfect life?

2. Think about a time when God's grace was evident in your life. What did that mean to you? Now think about three people who need to hear about that grace. How can you share that with them?

3. Sometimes we can be our own worst enemies when it comes to our flaws. What does it mean to you to realize that God loves *you* in spite of your imperfections?

4. Despite the fact that Cindy's pin was flawed, it was still useful. How can you take the scars of your life and use them for God?

TEN

The Birthstone

Each month of the year has been assigned a special jewel. Ancient people believed that wearing a birthstone brought good luck. To them, each stone represented a unique character trait: constancy for the garnet (January), innocence for the diamond (April), and contentment for the ruby (July). During the Middle Ages, people thought that wearing such stones would keep them from harm. Although such superstitions are not usually heeded today, many women still enjoy collecting jewelry with a special gem that marks their birth month.

The picture you have of yourself,
your self-esteem, will have a profound
effect on the way you see the world
and the way your world sees you.

—*Earl Nightingale*

CHOSEN JUST FOR YOU

Ruby red, sapphire blue, emerald green. Brilliant colors flashing on a birthstone chart. Some scholars surmise that the tradition of assigning a birthstone can be traced back to the shining bejeweled breastplate worn by Aaron, big brother to mighty Moses (see Exodus 28). Aaron wore those twelve gems over his heart to show how precious the children of Israel were to God.

Before the world was made, God marked the date of your birth. Think of that. He recognized *you* in the womb, formed your fragile figure. You are His handmade treasure. Known and loved before you ever made a sound, before your own tiny heart began its steady beat.

Today as you look through your jewelry box, you may find a shiny birthstone set in a ring, necklace, or twinkling in a bright bracelet. Even as you look ahead to your next birthday celebration, realize that it's you who is priceless. The jewelry itself matters little—you are the one-of-a-kind gem.

Some of you had a rough beginning. Perhaps you fought to fill your lungs for the first time. Maybe you were born too early. Even today you could have lingering health concerns that stem from a difficult start. And yet you have overcome obstacles and your strength has abounded because God made you a fighter. A child of victory. Your birthstone jewelry commemorates your struggle, highlighting the precious gift of life.

Days can be difficult. You will be passed over for

promotions. Friends will make hurtful false assumptions. Someone will hit your car and "forget" to leave a note. However, for each ding and heartbreak, there will be moments of pure joy. Times when you cannot help but smile and thank God for loving you. Look for those God glimpses in everyday occurrences.

In God we have new birth. His grace renews and remakes us. If your childhood was spotted with tears, you might still question your value. Especially if you base your self-worth on the displeasure coloring another's eyes.

Look beyond your past. Focus instead on God's compassionate face. He holds a book, the Book of Life, and in it He has carefully noted your arrival. By choosing the month of your birth, He has in essence assigned you a special stone to mark the occasion.

See the sparkle God placed in your birthstone, the shine that glows within you. He shapes your soul and rejoices at every stage of your growth. He weeps with you in struggles, uplifts you in pain, and answers your fervent prayers. When you need a hand of hope, you need only reach out.

Mark every birthday with joy, remembering that God personally chose your birthstone as a sweet remembrance of His daily love.

Before I formed thee in the belly I knew thee;
and before thou camest forth out of the womb
I sanctified thee.

—*Jeremiah 1:5*

Lord, please help me to grasp how precious I am in the Savior's sight. How awesome it is to know you knew me and loved me even before I was born. Sometimes I get bogged down when looking at my past and I forget about the hope of a future with you. Remind me that each moment is a precious gift from God. Help me to make my birthday a time for sweet reflection, an occasion when joy always outweighs sorrow. Let every memory of my special day bring with it a sincere smile and a lilting laugh. Amen.

THE JEWELRY INSURANCE INVENTORY FORM

What is your treasure?

1. What are some of your favorite birthday memories? What are some of your favorite *spiritual* birthday memories?

2. Have you ever thought about how God loved us even before we were born? How does that make you feel? How can you show God that you love Him in return?

3. Gifts are an important part of birthdays. God excels at giving. Make a list of some of the gifts God has shared with you, and then spend time thanking Him.

4. Tell your children and grandchildren their stories. Whether adopted or born into your family, help them see your delight in them. And then share your spiritual story. When and where did you meet Jesus? Were there special times when God provided for your needs? What other faith-related experiences can you share?

ELEVEN

Grandpa's Pocket Watch

The first pocket watches stretched the seams of a pocket. You might think of these beauties as the transitional timepieces between full-sized windup clocks and the sleek banded watches of the modern era. They were invented in the sixteenth century, and with each passing year they became smaller and more useful. The first pocket watches had only an hour hand. Pocket watches often had a chain so the well-dressed wearer could attach them to a vest, belt, coat, or lapel. Fobs—a short leather piece to protect the crystal—later became the fashion.

Lost time is never found again.

—*Benjamin Franklin*

WHOSE TIME IS IT ANYWAY?

Today if you see a pocket watch, you can be assured there is a story behind the artful carved decorations on the watch cover. Maybe it was a wedding gift from a new father-in-law with the strong reminder, *Treasure my daughter every minute of every day.*

Perhaps a young man worked overtime for months to squirrel away a few pennies to purchase it, one of his first proud investments after journeying from another land. Or maybe his beloved dad gave it to him as a way of saying, *Congratulations on making it into college. Now spend a few hours studying.* And, of course, there's the timeless tradition of getting the proverbial gleaming gold pocket watch upon retiring after decades of service.

Pocket watches served many a unique purpose for those who were lucky enough to own or inherit one. They were handheld reminders of the importance of good habits. Each day the owner had to take the time to wind it. Seemed like a simple thing—remembering to turn the watch stem to reset the spring works and keep it ticking steadily. But he had to be careful not to overwind the pocket watch, or the mechanism would break. Winding the pocket watch each morning became an important, if mundane, duty. A small regular responsibility that, if missed, could have serious repercussions.

How many other small, simple things do we try to do and yet find surprisingly difficult? Think of it. Do we exercise each day? Eat right at every meal? Floss each night before bed? Pray and read God's Word regularly? Say I love you to those who are precious in our lives? Honestly, it's a challenge to simply do what we know we must and to keep at such tasks faithfully.

If we forget to keep the spring wound on our pocket watch, its thin hands creak to a stop. It no longer serves any purpose. We're like that too. We have the best of intentions to dwell on and memorize Scripture and to put our Lord first, but somehow we find it difficult to follow through. Distractions divert us. Sometimes we feel just like that little round pocket clock—unattended and unable to serve its valuable function.

The beautiful thing about a stopped watch is that the situation is quickly and easily remedied. We don't have to leave Gramps's gleaming timepiece quiet on the dresser. All it takes is a purposeful action on our part, and we can get it ticking again. Similarly, if we've forgotten to check in with God lately—the great watchmaker—all we have to do is bow our hearts and make the connection anew.

But, beloved, be not ignorant of this one thing,
that one day is with the Lord as a thousand years,
and a thousand years as one day.

—*2 Peter 3:8*

*You know me, Lord. My good intentions outnumber
the hours of my busy day. Make me stop, like a silent
watch, and think. Remind me that you have given me
a precious life but limited time. When I look backward,
it's as though the decades have rushed by like a roar-
ing river. Events anticipated soon become long-ago
memories. Please help me to see that every minute
matters. Let me use my hours and days in meaningful
service to you, full of the joy that you grant fresh each
and every morning. Amen.*

THE JEWELRY INSURANCE INVENTORY FORM

What is your treasure?

1. As the days and years zoom by, are you keeping track of your time so you can accomplish things for Him, or are you sidetracked? Jot down three things you'd like to do for God.

2. Do you fear the passage of time? How would you live differently if you knew you only had three weeks or months to live? Reflect on this topic and write down a few thoughts.

3. When's the last time you admired the complexity of the works inside a watch? Take a look at what the human mind can create—and then consider the God who made that mind. How can you use your mind (and your talents) for God?

4. Are you spending enough time with God? Set aside some quiet time today and hear what He has to say to you.

TWELVE

Earrings

Sorry, ladies. The guys had the idea first. Historically speaking, the earliest earrings adorned men of Assyria and Egypt to let others know they had arrived and had the wealth to own such bulky bejeweled treasures. But women quickly caught up and became the primary collectors of earring options. At first glance, earrings seem like strange baubles. But well-chosen bits of jewelry accent the shape and beauty of the face, and the movement of certain earrings draws attention to the wearer's uniqueness and sense of style.

The best part of beauty
is that which no picture can express.
—Francis Bacon

EARRINGS THAT LAST

The baby stared, long lashes blinking. The large round hoop of gold dangled and jangled, and the little one grabbed on with a pudgy fist. Yank! He held on tight. Baby didn't mean to squeeze and twist and pull your ear, but he sure enjoyed your surprised reaction.

That's one thing about earrings. You've really got to mean it when you choose to make that first hole—or your latest. That's because the typical piercing changes your lobe or any number of standard sites. And that alteration becomes permanent. No matter what location you choose, you want to be sure that the earrings are firmly attached. How many times have you retraced your tracks looking for a loose earring that decided to dive for the dirt?

There are, of course, options to pierced ears. Remember Grandma's clip-ons? Often heavy and made of weighty metals, they pulled the poor lobe down toward the ground, but they were easily removed. If the clip-on earrings were backed with a second small clip, they weren't going anywhere unless you chose to remove them.

Earrings come in an endless variety. Some are made of precious stones, wood, or beads. You can find a beautiful pair for a few bucks at a garage sale or spend thousands on diamonds that sparkle by candlelight, but wherever you find them, they're usually purchased by the pair.

A young woman writing a paper hauled piles of books to her table in the library. Hours later, she felt an itch and

◆ ◆

pulled her ear. One of her diamond earrings was missing! They'd been a gift from her parents. Frantic, she ran to the stacks and looked everywhere, opening and closing volumes, hoping her tiny treasure had been caught in one of them. She returned many times for one more look but without success.

In a similar situation, think about the Good Shepherd who lost one precious lamb and searched until He found it. Rejoice! Our Shepherd *never* gives up on us.

In Bible times, when Rome ruled the earth, those who chose to wholeheartedly serve their masters were called bondservants. Part of the process of giving yourself body and soul to another meant piercing an ear with an awl, a tool that made a small hole (Exodus 21:5–6). Such servants no longer were their own. By their act they stated—and showed—their devotion to another. And the unadorned piercing made the point yet more obvious.

Think about the connection you have to the Lord. Is your connection with Him as evident as an earring? Are you fastened tightly to Him? Determine to stay hooked into the Father, embedded into a welcoming Christian faith community, and locked securely to the source of all hope and joy.

◆ ◆

Deck thyself now with majesty and excellency;
and array thyself with glory and beauty.
—Job 40:10

Oh Lord, there are so many reminders of you in the simple and complex things in our lives. Help us to think about how an earring can symbolize sacrificing our dreams and desires for another. Make us bondservants of the heart to our Lord, to our beloved family, and to the friends we care for deeply. Serving you is never a burden. And when we see a shiny trinket twinkling on a God-formed ear, let us smile. Thank you for the beauty all around us, on display for us to cherish—if we will but take a moment to look. Amen.

THE JEWELRY INSURANCE INVENTORY FORM

What is your treasure?

1. Nobody likes losing one earring. It usually happens because we didn't have it fastened well. When we're not fastened well to God, we lose our close relationship with Him. What do you think is needed for us to be connected tightly to God?

2. Back in Bible days, wearing an earring meant that you'd become a bondservant to someone and that you no longer belonged to yourself. How does that apply to us spiritually?

3. Think of someone who is a spiritual giant to you. What makes her life beautiful? What traits does she possess that you'd like to have in your own spiritual journey?

4. Earrings are often given as Christmas or birthday gifts. When's the last time you shared about God's gift of salvation with someone? Ask God to place somebody on your heart today.

THIRTEEN

Sentimental Items

Sentimental items are things that have touched us emotionally. They remind us of precious moments spent together, special times in our lives, or occasions we want to remember. Sentimental items are usually things that wouldn't mean much to anyone else—but they sure do mean a lot to us. They often have little monetary value, but we think they're priceless because they represent something or someone we love or a special time in our lives.

Just as our children are precious to us,
we are precious to the Father,
who calls us His jewels.
—*Michelle Cox*

PRICELESS JEWELS

I posted on Facebook recently and asked folks to tell me what was in their jewelry boxes. According to their responses, there are enough baby teeth stored there to make dentures for all of New York. It seems we've discovered where the tooth fairy drops leftover teeth after she's finished with them.

Plastic or satin bags filled with teeth probably aren't one of the first things that come to mind when you think of your jewelry box, but it makes perfect sense since jewelry boxes are where we keep things that are precious to us.

And what's more precious than family?

That's why moms keep those first tiny teeth. They're sweet memories of snaggletoothed smiles from a beloved child and markers that our kids are growing up, whether we like it or not.

Baby teeth aren't the only family-related items in jewelry boxes. Many of us keep the hospital bracelets we clipped from the arms of our newborns when we brought them home from the hospital—precious reminders of the day our life and family changed forever.

And what about those cherished locks of hair in jewelry boxes? I remember snipping pieces of oh-so-soft hair from my little guys—and I still have the envelopes with locks of hair that my mother kept from my sister and me.

Some moms have booties or other items that were made by their grandmothers, tiny stuffed animals, or special photos.

Others have love letters with crooked letters and misspelled words from their children.

Whether it's baby teeth or hospital bracelets or some other keepsake, the possibilities of cherished items to store in our jewelry boxes—our treasure chests—are endless.

They are all mementos of precious times in our lives. And you know what? I can look through my Bible—God's treasure chest of sweet promises—and discover mementos of cherished moments there as well.

There are dozens of underlined verses and passages of Scripture, moments where God whispered sweet peace to me, gave me strength for tough times, or highlighted something in my life that I needed to change.

When I've faced difficult times, those precious promises from God's Word have arrived in my mind and heart just as I have needed them.

There are notes in the margins of my Bible where He gave me fresh insight into His Word, things I'd never noticed before that provided new glimpses of Him.

There are dates and the letters TP, which stand for "tried and proven," from seemingly impossible prayers that I prayed—and He answered.

A mother keeping her treasures in her jewelry box. A Father keeping sweet promises—far more priceless than jewels—in His Word. Yes, what could be more precious than family?

A book of remembrance was written before him for them that feared the LORD, and that thought upon his name. And they shall be mine, saith the LORD of hosts, in that day when I make up my jewels.

—*Malachi 3:16–17*

Dear Father, you have blessed me far more than I've deserved. Thank you for the priceless gift of my family and for all the cherished moments you've given us together through the years. I'm so grateful to be your beloved child, and it boggles my mind that you consider me one of your jewels. You have blessed me on so many occasions by sending that sweet unexplainable peace during difficult days. Thank you for all the times your Word has sparkled into my life, providing just what I needed when I needed it. Amen.

THE JEWELRY INSURANCE INVENTORY FORM

What is your treasure?

1. The items in a woman's jewelry box often reflect what's precious to her. Does your Bible reflect what is precious to you? Are the pages worn? Are verses underlined? And if you have children, do they see you reading your Bible and praying?

2. What are some of your favorite passages or verses of Scripture? Why are they precious to you?

3. Your family is one of God's most precious gifts to you. Our lives are busy, and we can sometimes be overwhelmed by responsibilities. What are you doing to keep your focus on what's really important? What do you need to change to help you do that?

4. Take a few minutes and just page through your Bible. What treasures do you find there? What does God's Word mean to you? Have you shared that with your children?

FOURTEEN

Candy Jewelry

Candy makers have tried many new approaches to sell their goodies, including candy jewelry necklaces, bracelets, and rings. It's an amusing mix of style and good taste. Typically, the necklaces are made of hard candy that you can leave in its pristine state, or if you need a sugar boost, you can nip off a rounded bead and suck on it. Children love them because they can wear them as an accessory and have something good to nibble at the same time.

No matter what treasure
may give you great pleasure,
No precious sweet that you possess
will match the many ways you bless.

—John Perrodin

THE SWEETEST OF JEWELS

Candy jewelry is considered a novelty item, and for many wearers, a delicious treat. There's just something delightful about having a lip-smacking sweet treat within range of your mouth at all times. A homemade version is easily fashioned by looping small colorful candy rounds onto a long piece of string, tying it with a tight bow at the end, and you have a treat fit for a hungry princess (or greedy little prince).

Other types of candy jewelry include rings with big gaudy candy jewels or bracelets with tiny sugar beads. If you're lucky, you might also find softer, pliable gummy candies decorating a bracelet or fashioned into a sticky sapphire on the end of a candy rope.

This type of jewelry is notable because its only real purpose is to provide fun. It definitely wouldn't be a viable item for long-term storage in our jewelry boxes.

Wouldn't it be nice if there were more things in our lives that didn't matter? How different our demeanor would be if we weren't constantly worrying about the utilitarian purpose of every stitch of clothing we wear or berating ourselves for each empty calorie crossing our lips.

What a delight it is to give out an inexpensive treat that the children and grandchildren are sure to love. Ultimately, the necklace shortens as the children nibble at the tiny pieces of hard candy. How similar this is to many of our quickly purchased treasures. Even costly symbols of success fall by the wayside with disuse or overestimation of their value.

Think of the purchases of jewelry, shoes, handbags, or skirts of every length. Have they remained the must-have bargains we thought they would? These are fun, frivolous things—and that's fine from time to time—but when it comes to important choices spiritually, we should ask, what is it that matters for the kingdom of God?

Many of our treasures are nothing more than sticky, shiny objects: even that new car, those new kitchen appliances, or new pumps. Just a little something we picked up along the way. Perhaps the better course is to forgo a few eye-catching trinkets and invest in the souls of those around us—our children, grandchildren, nieces and nephews, neighbors, and friends. Those who are lost and sometimes don't even know it.

Candy necklaces are fun, silly, and even tasty in a sickly sweet sort of way. But they won't last forever. They're not meant to. When it comes to collecting spiritual treasures (the ones that will *really* last), let's be intentional about filling our jewelry boxes with the pearls of great price and the golden gifts of faith that have lasting value.

Lay not up for yourselves treasures upon earth,
where moth and rust doth corrupt, and where thieves
break through and steal: But lay up for yourselves treasures in heaven, where neither moth nor rust
doth corrupt, and where thieves do not break through
nor steal: For where your treasure is, there will
your heart be also.

—Matthew 6:19–21

Oh God, please give me discernment as I strive to make wise decisions about the finite volume of time and money you have given me to steward. Sometimes I find myself chasing after trends and hoping that I'll find something that will bring lasting happiness. Often I end up making purchases—the equivalent of useless candy jewelry—that don't satisfy my heart. Instead, I get stuff that fills my closet and crowds my soul. Show me something about simplicity and truth each and every day. Let me not be afraid to appropriately dispose of the unneeded and unnecessary as I make room in my heart and my treasure box for what has true and lasting value. Amen.

THE JEWELRY INSURANCE INVENTORY FORM

What is your treasure?

1. Candy jewelry is for children. Just as we mature from children to adults, we should mature spiritually. Are you a grown-up Christian or are you stuck at an immature level in your faith journey?

2. Is your life out of control? When things become out of balance, it affects us physically, emotionally, and spiritually. List some things that are stressing you today. Ask God what changes you need to make.

3. Candy jewelry (or any candy) can be a temptation. It's the same with our spiritual lives. Satan knows where we are vulnerable, and he attacks us there. Make a list of your weaknesses. Being forewarned will help you to be forearmed.

4. Nobody takes a moving van to heaven with them, yet we often work to accumulate treasures that don't matter. What treasures can you heap up for eternity?

FIFTEEN

The Wristwatch

A wristwatch is a small timepiece that is worn on a band and strapped around the wrist. There are many choices available, with silver, gold, or leather for the watchbands, and diamonds or other decorations providing bling to the watch. Watch faces can come in a variety of sizes and shapes. Although wristwatches are decorative items, they serve the purpose of helping us keep track of the minutes and hours of our lives. When the battery runs down or the watch isn't wound, it quits doing its job.

It is the heart that makes a man rich.
He is rich according to what he is,
not according to what he has.

—Henry Ward Beecher

THE REAL DEAL

After his grandfather's death, my fifteen-year-old son, Jason, discovered a special item while we were going through Dad's possessions. "I didn't know Paw Paw had a Rolex. Can I have it?"

I looked at the watch in question. I didn't remember my dad having a Rolex. Surely he would have mentioned it if he'd bought one. I racked my brain for all that I knew about Rolex watches. I knew they were expensive and had a reputation for their performance and reliability.

I told Jason, "Let's do some research." We compared Dad's watch to the website images. The emblem was exactly the same. Every other detail matched. I couldn't imagine Dad spending that much on a watch, but the chance was always there.

Jason asked, "Can I wear it?"

"Just be careful with it until somebody can check it out."

At school the next day, Jason's friends quickly noticed his new watch. "Dude, is that a *Rolex*?" was the question he heard over and over.

Not long after that, I took the watch to the finest jeweler in town. That's where things got interesting. I told the jeweler how we'd found the watch, expecting him to take one look at it and deem it fake.

Instead he looked at it and said, "It looks like a real Rolex." He gave it a close examination with his eyepiece. Detail after detail matched. After an extensive inspection, he found one thing about the inner workings of the watch that a real Rolex wouldn't have—but it was so close to the real thing that even he had trouble deciding if it was real or fake.

Girlfriends, that fake Rolex is a great lesson for us. Are we the real deal as Christians, or are we a cheap imitation? When others look at us, do they see a woman who's sold out to God, or do they see someone pretending to walk with Him?

More importantly, what does God see when He looks at the inner workings of our hearts? That's what's truly important. Just as a watch needs a battery, let's charge our spiritual batteries by reading His Word and spending time in prayer. Just as a watch needs to be wound so that it will keep working, let's get wound up with joy about serving Him.

Our watches are on display around our wrists for everyone to see, and they help us keep track of time. Are we wearing Jesus—putting Him on display for a world that needs to know about Him? Are we spending our hours and days on things that don't really matter?

The world is full of imitation watches and imitation Christians. Let's determine today that we'll be the real deal for Him, valuable and known for our performance and reliability.

See then that ye walk circumspectly,
not as fools, but as wise, redeeming the time,
because the days are evil.
—*Ephesians 5:15–16*

Dear God, there are so many hypocrites—fakes—in this world, and I don't want to be one of them. I want to be the real deal for you. When you look at the inner workings of my heart, I hope you find a woman whose heart longs to serve you. Help me to read my Bible and pray so that I can keep my spiritual batteries charged. Thank you for loving me and for looking at someone like me and seeing a beautiful creation of inestimable value. Amen.

THE JEWELRY INSURANCE INVENTORY FORM

What is your treasure?

1. God looks at our hearts. He knows when we're the real deal and when we aren't. What does God see when He looks at *your* heart? What would you like Him to see?

2. Folks display their expensive watches on their wrists. Are we on display for God, presenting an example that will lead others to Him?

3. Just as people wind their watches to keep them working, we need time in God's Word and in prayer to keep our spiritual lives ticking away. Are you spending enough time with Him, or are your spiritual batteries worn down?

4. So many people are going through rough times. They're looking for hope, looking for something—or somebody—that's real. When others look at you and how you live your life, what do they see?

SIXTEEN

The Medical Alert Bracelet

A medical alert bracelet is an unassuming basic tool for survival when the unexpected happens. It is worn on the wrist so if emergency medical care is needed the arriving EMT has a brief snapshot of the patient's medical history. Marked on one side with an obvious symbol of the staff of Asclepius, the universal sign for medicine, the reverse side is engraved with a succinct list of details about the person's medical issues. This simple piece of jewelry can save a life.

Flowers are lovely; Love is flower-like;
Friendship is a sheltering tree.
—Samuel T. Coleridge

IMPORTANT ACCESSORY

The smallest decision can have the greatest impact. I think back to first grade when a young lady held out her hand and asked to borrow one of my brand-new crayons. "Please," she said with a gap-toothed smile. I felt nervous and honestly didn't want to give up a single one of my pristine colors with their perfect tips. But I grudgingly remembered what Mom always said about sharing and gave in.

A single day can change a life in other ways as well. Another friend of mine, Betty Jane, was at a Fourth of July barbeque. She stumbled as she walked to her seat. Betty's full plate tipped, and she spilled some salad. I wondered what had tripped her.

Fortunately, she seemed to catch herself, and I saw how embarrassed she was. We all know the feeling. Not wanting to draw attention to her mortification, I turned away and engaged another companion in an excited conversation about grandchildren. I forgot all about Betty's bumble.

But then I saw people standing, huddled around someone. I ran to the crowd. It was Betty. Something was wrong. "Call 911," a man shouted. It was her husband. His lips were at her cheek, telling her not to worry, but fear was etched into his features. I stood watching, concerned for my friend. Bowing my head, I prayed for Betty, feeling helpless as I observed the scene in front of me.

The ambulance came, and the EMT team lifted her onto a gurney. A man fiddled with something shiny around her wrist. A thin silver bracelet. What a blessing that she hadn't left it in her jewelry box that morning!

Thankfully, Betty survived with no long-term health concerns. That was due in large part to her smart decision to wear a bland silver medical alert bracelet that provided details about her medical history, drug allergies, and other vital health information. This plain piece of jewelry didn't exactly go with her fancy floral dress, but she didn't care. She knew it could save her life—and it did.

Spiritually speaking, do we sometime choose friends based on their outward appearance or their value as "accessories"? Do we select acquaintances who might help us climb the ladder in society or at work? Or are we comfortable with those who honor us with their loyalty and love even though they're not perfect—and know we aren't either?

With the wisdom time brings, I've learned that lasting relationships often arise from small, humble connections. Let's be thankful for those who enrich our lives without flashy show. Faithful friends who support us when the unthinkable happens. I don't know about you, but I'm grateful for those precious people who are there for us—praying for us—no matter what.

Pleasant words are as an honeycomb,
sweet to the soul, and health to the bones.

—*Proverbs 16:24*

Lord, we have no idea what this day holds. We can earnestly hope that everything will work out exactly as we plan, but how often does that happen? Sometimes we can tell when storms are coming in. We can sense changes in our health or that of a loved one, but we don't always heed the warnings. Please help us to be open to seeking assistance when you send us subtle—or quite obvious—signs. And teach us ways to improve our health so we're able to long enjoy opportunities to love and serve you—and those who are most precious to us. Amen.

THE JEWELRY INSURANCE INVENTORY FORM

What is your treasure?

1. When Betty had a health emergency, she was prepared with her medical alert bracelet. We can also encounter unexpected spiritual emergencies where we're blindsided by circumstances. What can you do to be prepared for those spiritual crisis moments?

2. Many of us ignore our health problems. How can that impact us physically, spiritually, and emotionally?

3. None of us know how many days God's given us. If you knew you'd meet Him in twenty-one days, what would you do differently in your life?

4. Friends are one of God's best gifts—and God is the best friend ever. Stop right now and pray for your friends. And then contact them to tell them how much they mean to you.

SEVENTEEN

Assorted Jewelry

An assortment of jewelry is a collection of jewelry that piles up in our jewelry boxes over the years, consisting of inexpensive jewelry, costly gems, souvenir jewelry from trips, and heirloom items. Some of it is stylish, and some of it went out of style years ago. Or sometimes we've quit wearing it because our taste changed. Other pieces are kept because they were gifts or they have sentimental value. But all of it was chosen with love and care.

God made each of us unique,
and there is a vast mystery and beauty
surrounding the human soul.
—Alan Loy McGinnis

What's in Your Jewelry Box?

Do you have an assortment of jewelry in your jewelry box? I hadn't really thought about it before, but our jewelry choices change throughout our lifetimes.

My little granddaughters have tiny earrings, inexpensive rings, and Disney and cartoon-themed jewelry. They might even have some candy necklaces in their jewelry boxes.

They're little girls, and those are the kinds of things you'd expect to find there, but it would be odd for women to stock their jewelry boxes like that—although I must confess to having some Disney-themed jewelry that I wear when we make our trips there.

Styles change over the years, and our jewelry choices change with them according to color palates, silver vs. gold, classic vs. funky pieces, long chains vs. short chains, delicate vs. statement pieces, items that will match our outfits, and personal preferences.

And sometimes our jewelry choices change because of funny reasons. My husband and I were on a short trip recently. I had a dressy event to attend the week after that and didn't have jewelry for my dress, so on the way home, we stopped at one of those huge stores that has nothing but jewelry. I love how they arrange the displays by colors, but sometimes it's overwhelming. I've found it helps me to focus on finding jewelry for just one or two outfits when I'm there.

I found several sets of matching necklaces and earrings that I thought would work with my semiformal attire, so I walked over to a mirror to try them on to make sure they'd fit the neckline of the dress.

One of the necklaces had just the right amount of sparkle, was a great fit for the design on my dress, and had a delicate gold chain. And that's where I discovered the problem. I realized that while the smaller-style necklace was beautiful, it didn't look good on me. Yes, I've reached the age where delicate necklaces don't cover up the wrinkles under my turkey neck. It's really bad when the chain disappears into your wrinkles!

But you know what I'm grateful for today? Our jewelry choices (and many other things) might change, but God is always the same. He never goes out of style. He's always a perfect fit.

You know what's really awesome? We were *chosen* by Him. I might find it challenging when going through those mega jewelry stores, but God has never had a problem with making decisions. He looked into a sea of humanity and He said, *That one! That's my girl.*

Sometimes we're guilty of looking at ourselves and saying things like, "I'm old. I'm ugly. I mess up everything I touch. I'm worthless." The next time Satan whispers that to you, just remind him you're a one-of-a-kind chosen jewel in God's jewelry box.

For thou art an holy people unto the Lord thy God:
the Lord thy God hath chosen thee to be
a special people unto himself, above all people
that are upon the face of the earth.

—Deuteronomy 7:6

Sometimes I'm my own worst enemy, Lord. I know you don't make junk, and yet I'm often the first one to tear myself down. Sometimes I believe the lies of others, even those I call friends and family—those who should be lifting me up, not tearing me down. Help me remember that you see me as one of your valuable jewels, as someone you can use for your purposes and plan—despite my flaws. I'm so grateful that in a world where things are constantly changing, I can count on you to always be the same. Amen.

THE JEWELRY INSURANCE INVENTORY FORM

What is your treasure?

1. Just as we do inventory of our jewelry boxes, we also need to take inventory of our hearts. What do you need to purge from there?

2. Our jewelry choices change over the years, and our spiritual journeys change as well. Find some quiet time where you can listen for direction. Ask God to open your heart and mind. Jot down what you hear from Him.

3. What does it mean to you to know we have an unchanging God? What kind of security does that give you?

4. Sometimes we're our own worst enemies. Satan knows exactly what to whisper in our ears to defeat us—but God *chose* us. Write this down: *[Your name] was chosen by God. He has a purpose and a plan for [your name].* How does that give you confidence?

EIGHTEEN

The Engagement Ring

Though rarely found in the jewelry box because it's never taken off, the engagement ring is a treasure. It's a circle of precious metal (often set with jewels) worn on the finger. The ring is given by the groom-to-be and signifies the couple's betrothal. Most young women dream of falling in love and the day when the man of their dreams will give them an engagement ring. She wears the ring as a sign of their love and a visible reminder of their commitment to each other.

God proved His love on the cross.
When Christ hung, and bled, and died,
it was God saying to the world, "I love you."

—Billy Graham

For most women, it's a day they've dreamed about since they were a little girl playing dress-up, waiting for their handsome prince to arrive. You know what day I'm talking about—the one where the prince pulls out a ring box and pops that "Will you marry me?" question.

I remember the day my son, Jason, proposed to his girl-friend, Kella. Our family was on vacation at Hilton Head Island, a place that's been special to all of us. When Jason bought the engagement ring, he decided to propose on the beach at sunset with the Harbour Town Lighthouse in the background. On that particular day, he suggested to Kella that they go take some pictures of the lighthouse while the sun set.

Jason placed the camera on the tripod, and using the timer delay, the two posed for photos. Right before he proposed, Jason switched the dial to video, and then he walked over, got down on one knee, and asked Kella to marry him.

The video is so sweet as it captured their excitement ... and Jason swatting at his head, arms, and legs as the sand fleas attacked him. It was an unexpected part of the proposal and a funny moment in a day they'll remember forever.

Engagement rings are one of the most special pieces of jewelry that will ever be in a woman's jewelry box. Sometimes they aren't expensive, but they are a priceless symbol of a love commitment between two individuals.

I vividly remember wearing my new engagement ring,

twisting my hand in the sunlight to watch the ring sparkle. Showing my ring to our family and friends was so exciting. Paul and I were in love, and I wanted everyone to know about it.

And that leads to some important questions for all of us to consider: Are we that excited when it comes to sharing about God's love for us? Do we put our faith on display for others to see?

A prospective groom doesn't give the love of his life a ring from the bubble-gum machine. He saves his money and buys something valuable and precious. He pays a price for it, and he gives something that will last a lifetime.

That's exactly what God did. He paid the ultimate price for us—and we can count on it to endure the test of time.

A woman with an engagement ring as a symbol of her fiance's love; a God who wore a crown of thorns as a symbol of His love for us—both are priceless displays of love for all the world to see.

You said I will to your handsome prince. Have you said I will to the one who loves you with a perfect love? That's a decision you will never regret.

◆ ◆

Yea, I have loved thee
with an everlasting love.
—*Jeremiah 31:3*

I was lost in sin, Lord, but you loved me anyway. That kind of love overwhelms me, and I am grateful beyond words for the gift you gave me in your Son. Thank you for paying the price for me. Thank you for a love that will last a lifetime and for the security of knowing that I will always have you in my life, come what may. Father, just as I showed off my engagement ring for everyone to see, give me boldness to share my faith in such a manner that others will see the sparkle of your love. Amen.

◇ ◇

THE JEWELRY INSURANCE INVENTORY FORM

What is your treasure?

1. The proposal is one of the most anticipated and exciting days in a young woman's life. It's a moment when two sweethearts pledge their lives to one another. How do you think that applies to our spiritual lives?

2. An engagement ring is a symbol of love and commitment. It's meant to last "until death do us part." How has God's love for you impacted your life? How does it affect you to know that you'll spend eternity with God?

3. Who can you think of who needs to hear about that love? How could you share that message with them?

4. God gave His all for us—and all He asks in return is for our hearts. Take a few minutes today and tell Him what He means to you.

NINETEEN

Costume Jewelry

For hundreds of years, costume jewelry has served as a unique cultural barometer. In previous centuries, the gems in such pieces were made of glass, and then semi-precious stones became readily available. This meant that jewelry could appear fancier while still remaining accessible to commoners with little money to spare. Costume jewelry brought timeless beauty to the middle class. It was no longer only nobility who could afford to wear bejeweled master-pieces. Anyone could.

Whatever beauty you choose to wear only
highlights the Creator's genius and flair.

—*John Perrodin*

JEWELS FOR ALL

Once upon a time a rich royal family fell upon hard circumstances. They had to discharge most of their servants, sell their horses, and cut back on the quality of their possessions. Tragically, they were also forced to sell their most precious jewelry to keep the creditors at bay. To save face, they had a master craftsman create replacement necklaces, bracelets, and rings with gems made of glass, exactly like those they had parted with. Though they sparkled still, they were not valuable like the one-of-a-kind originals.

Through the years, women have admired and wished for beautiful jewelry like that worn by royalty or by legendary beauties such as Elizabeth Taylor, Jackie Kennedy-Onassis, Audrey Hepburn, and Princess Diana. But of course they could never afford such priceless baubles. So costume jewelry took its place as an accepted and enjoyable alternative for the rest of us.

Many pieces of costume jewelry are based on famous settings worn by the rich and famous. Some styles are playful and outlandish, while others are understated and elegant.

Though you sport pearls, everyone knows you're not really wearing the breathtaking triple-strand necklace that Barbara Bush modeled at her husband's inauguration. (Did you know that even *her* pearls were costume jewelry?)

Reflect for a moment on the pearl of great price from Scripture. It was no cheap fake. In our mind's eye we probably picture it as shimmering and huge. The merchant, who would definitely know perfection if he saw it, went searching for beauty beyond measure. Something special. The likes of which he had never seen before. "Who, when he had found one pearl of great price, went and sold all that he had, and bought it" (Matthew 13:46).

You are that stunning pearl—the treasure God has been seeking. You are worth everything to Him. You were purchased by the Father at the cost of His dear Son's life.

When you use costume jewelry to complete an outfit, you express your own unique blend of creativity. It's a delight to use your imagination and play dress-up ... even if you're an adult. But no matter who you are on the outside—or pretend to be—it's what is on the inside that really matters. We know that, but we don't always believe our own eyes.

At the end of the day when you take off the fancy trinkets and look in the mirror, who do you see? Look again at the amazing person before you. Observe your unadorned beauty. Know that you are an amazing creation handmade by God. And bask in your Maker's smile.

In like manner also, that women adorn themselves
in modest apparel, with shamefacedness
and sobriety; not with ... costly array.

—*1 Timothy 2:9*

Lord, please help me not to take myself so seriously. It's my tendency sometimes to squeeze out every drop of meaning from small day-to-day happenings— to overanalyze someone's words or questioning look. Instead, I need to take things at face value, not worry so much, and enjoy my brief time on this amazing planet. If someone slights me, then show me how to forgive quickly. If I feel hurt by being left out or ignored, let me remember to rest in you. When I look at myself and see someone of little worth—like inexpensive costume jewelry in a jewelry box filled with costly gems—remind me that I'm loved by the God who made the universe and that you think I'm beautiful and valuable. Amen.

THE JEWELRY INSURANCE INVENTORY FORM

What is your treasure?

1. Back in the day, members of royalty had imitations made of jewelry they had to sell. We do something similar when we pretend all is perfect in our world. How is that harmful to us personally and to others?

2. For many centuries, women have longed for expensive jewelry—but do we set our target just as high when it comes to our faith? What goals could you set for things to accomplish for God?

3. Those members of royalty had fake jewels made so people wouldn't know they were poor. Why do we care so much about what others think? Are we as concerned about what God thinks?

4. How much time do you spend on your beauty routine, getting dressed and accessorized each day? How much time do you spend each day on beautifying your soul?

TWENTY

The Wedding Ring

Wedding bands are another "always on hand" treasure. Traditionally they are made of shining yellow gold, though some couples prefer other metals like silver, platinum, or white gold. A wedding ring is placed upon the fourth finger of the left hand during the sacred ceremony. Whether you had a full church affair or a small service before a few friends, the shining bands you and your husband carefully slipped on represented a vow of faithfulness and a promise of everlasting love. Like the ring, your love will hopefully have no end.

Marriage is a refining process God uses to make us into the kind of person He wants us to be.

—*Anonymous*

A Glimmering Reminder

The wedding ring truly means something special. For many women, that metallic band is her most priceless possession, not because of its monetary value but because of its eternal significance. The smooth circular rings that the bride and groom give to each other represent life eternal. They have no starting point and no conclusion.

The glowing bride symbolizes the stunning bride of Christ: the church. The marriage vow is a reminder that one day Jesus will come back to take His church—His forgiven people—to a glorious mansion in heaven to rejoice forever at the wedding feast.

You may be satisfied in your singleness, hoping to share your life, or engaged to an amazing man. You could be a starry-eyed newlywed, or maybe you've been crazy in love for decades. Regardless of your status, the wedding ring should make you stop and stare. That's because it serves as a glimmering reminder of who *you* are in Christ and the esteem with which the holy Bridegroom holds you. Regardless of your marital status, no earthly trials can ever displace your position as the beloved bride of Jesus.

What else makes the ring so special? It often boasts an engraved date or short phrase expressing lifetime love. With rare exceptions, this ring stays on your left ring finger, which is traditionally believed to have a vein, the vena amoris, which connects straight to the heart. That's why your engagement ring—no matter how stunning—is placed closer

◆ ◆

to your fingertip while the wedding ring stays closest to your heart. What a wonderful reminder of the love that binds you.

The ring itself represents a circle with no beginning or end, but there is far more to that imagery. Reflect also that the wearer resides within a precious sphere of protection. No forces or influences that might unravel your vows should ever be brought inside that small circle meant only for two. Neither partner should ever venture outside that intimate space to seek comfort and emotional strength from another. Such actions could damage the very soul of your marriage.

Some see a wedding ring as a mere bit of jewelry, an accessory, not a lifelong pledge. Something to be removed as the mood strikes. Look at your tiny reflection shimmering like a gem on the flat edge of your wedding ring, and take an inventory of what's most important to you. That plain holy band should mean the world to you.

God—your Bridegroom—wants to be your love for a lifetime. The next time you stroke your fingers across the smoothness of your wedding ring, take a minute to thank Him for the spouse He's blessed you with, and then thank Him for the oh-so-precious privilege of having Him choose *you* to be His bride.

Let us be glad and rejoice, and give honour to him:
for the marriage of the Lamb is come,
and his wife hath made herself ready.

—*Revelation 19:7*

Lord, thank you for marriage. Mine is not perfect, but it is still priceless, and I ask you to help me do all that I can to build upon the foundation that my spouse and I have laid. If improvements and renovations are necessary, please show me how to lead by serving and love by example. For those of us who are not married but seek to be, please create the connections and links that will allow holy marriage vows to be spoken in earnest and in your perfect timing. I know that I need never doubt that you have ordained this precious union between man and woman. Amen.

THE JEWELRY INSURANCE INVENTORY FORM

What is your treasure?

1. A wedding ring is a circle that has no beginning and no end. Why is that important in a marriage, and what are the spiritual applications of that symbolism?

2. We take vows on our wedding day, but people often break those promises as if they don't matter. Why are those words so important, and how does keeping (or breaking) them forever impact our lives, families, and our relationship with God?

3. A wedding ring represents a commitment of marriage between the bride and her groom. What can you do to keep that sacred trust? What safeguards can you set in place to protect your marriage?

4. When's the last time you prayed for your spouse or prayed together as a couple? Make a list of ways you can pray for your husband and commit to do just that.

TWENTY-ONE

A Locket

Unless we share its contents, no one knows for sure what treasure is bound within. That's the beauty of the locket. It can hold a tiny photo of a baby or a picture of a beloved husband. It's up to us what we hide in that small frame. We can exalt anything we choose. Our treasure is someone we value, a person who brings great joy. A pretty little locket lets us highlight someone we truly love. And often those lockets are discovered in an inherited jewelry box and valued even more because they've been passed down from one generation to another.

The smiling faces of our loved ones
reflect the treasures of our heart.

—John Perrodin

The intricate locket looked like a petite lantern. Braided metal decorated four delicate frames. When opened, there was a tiny central photo and then a miniscule frame that flipped upward, another that opened to the right, and a third that expanded to the left. From the viewer's vantage point, all four childish faces could be seen. If Sarah looked close enough (or held it far enough away!), she could just make out their sweet smiles, missing teeth, and freckles.

Sarah had treasured those photos when her husband had presented that special locket years ago, and now as a grandmother, the timeless pictures meant even more. How could she ever change out the pictures that came with this gift? They wordlessly captured a cherished moment in time when her sweet children had posed for a picture—knowing that their daddy was going to lock their images away in a gift for Mother's Day.

Fast-forward and two of her little flock are in their late twenties and have already presented her with beautiful blessings of their own. She adores the feel of them snuggled to her chest.

She can't help hoping for more grandchildren someday, but oh, what she'd give to go back in time for one more hour with the precious smiling faces in her beautiful bronze locket. Faces frozen in time but very much alive in her heart.

God also enjoys looking at the beaming faces of His children. In Scripture, God's chosen people are called the apple of His eye. The pupil was considered to be the core of the eye and therefore something to be zealously protected as it was required for sight and clear vision.

As the "apple of God's eye," we should consider ourselves deeply treasured. In Deuteronomy 32:10, the Bible says, "He found him in a desert land, and in the waste howling wilderness; he led him about, he instructed him, he kept him as the apple of his eye." Just as God saw the children of Jacob as precious in His sight, so does the doting mother view her own beautiful little ones. And her priceless locket is a special trove of treasure to her.

God holds us dear in His heart. Every time you snap open a special locket to view the face of your beloved, you can think of the way God holds you near as well. No matter what your past was like, your future in the Lord is bright and beautiful. You are loved and will be full of new hope if you'll only realize God has the most amazing design for you. Your life stands before the Maker as an amazing illumination in the locket of His heart. That's how special you are to Him today—and you always have been.

Again, the kingdom of heaven is like unto treasure
hid in a field; the which when a man hath found,
he hideth, and for joy thereof goeth and selleth
all that he hath, and buyeth that field.
—*Matthew 13:44*

Lord, the idea of a locket is so beautiful. I cherish the thought of holding pictures of precious loved ones close to my heart. We are a people who need reminders, and a locket tells us to stop and think about those who have been close to us through the years. You are the Creator of life and love and family, and I thank you for putting me exactly where you want me to be. Please open my eyes to the many miracles I can see in those around me. Show me how I can hold these treasured memories close. My connection with you makes my life worth living. I love you, Lord. Amen.

THE JEWELRY INSURANCE INVENTORY FORM

What is your treasure?

1. How does it make you feel to know that God holds your image close to His heart? How does that impact those moments when you put yourself down?

2. The Lord calls you "precious" and "beloved." Do you hear those words of affection and affirmation each and every day? Do you say them to others? Why or why not?

3. Sometimes we become bogged down by things that happened in our past, and they hinder us from moving forward to the future God has for us. What do you think God has in store for your future? Jot down three goals of things you'd like to do for Him.

4. How do you let your spouse, children, and friends know that you love them? How do you let God know you love Him? Through actions? Words? Spending time together?

TWENTY-TWO

The Purple Heart and Other Military Medals

Displayed proudly or kept in a felt-lined container for safekeeping within your jewelry box, the Purple Heart or other military awards appear to be nothing more than bits of burnished metal and colored ribbons. But what they stand for is priceless. Military medals visibly acknowledge inward courage, and they honor the brave people who have served our country. They include decorations and badges, each of which represents selfless service and loyal duty.

I only regret that I have but one life
to lose for my country.

—Nathan Hale

FOR LOVE OF COUNTRY

To be asked to watch over a soldier's military medals signifies that you have been significantly honored. You mean a great deal to the giver to be safekeeping such a treasure now. These remembrances take many forms. Whether it is one stripe on the left sleeve for every three years of service or one stripe on the right for every six months deployed to a combat zone, the symbol of service means far more than its component parts.

You might be the mother, wife, sweetheart, or sister of a military man (or it might have been you who served your country). A badge depicts recognition for a skill set like air assault, combat medical, combat action, expert field medical skills, and many others. The soldier's dedication and love of country are obvious.

Some of you (like my friend Adam Meister who humbly spoke with me about his Purple Hearts) may even possess a Purple Heart—the ultimate symbol of sacrifice, which is presented in the name of our nation's president. A soldier must have been injured or died fighting against the enemy. A Purple Heart can be earned multiple times but will only be issued once per military campaign or deployment. Look closely. If you see a star above President Washington's head, that represents multiple Purple Hearts given to the service member. For subsequent injuries, bronze and silver oak leaf clusters are granted as symbols of gratitude.

Our military lays down many personal freedoms and desires in order to serve. What integrity. What strength of character. These stalwart souls do not know when, and sometimes if, they will be coming back to their families. Or in what condition. As fellow citizens, we should be proud of those who have given up so much for us—in some cases even giving their lives for their country.

Jesus Christ laid down His life for all humanity. Though sinless, He experienced the pain of sin. Through His once-for-all sacrifice, we can live in complete assurance that heaven will one day be our home.

His sacrifice gives us life and freedom. And our military men and women protect that liberty, often at great cost. Whenever you take a moment to examine that Purple Heart or other military medal, close your eyes and picture the person who earned it. His or her bravery, perseverance, courage, and spirit keep us safe and secure.

That safety allows other freedoms—like sharing our faith—to take root and blossom. When we honor those we have lost, those injured, and those still serving strong, we are vividly reminded of what it means to put another first—and we can reflect anew on the sacrifice God made for us.

Greater love hath no man than this,
that a man lay down his life for his friends.
—*John 15:13*

O God of our fathers, thank you for giving us this land of hope and freedom. Thank you for the men and women who have, through the centuries, protected the high ideals and values that make this nation great. Lord, you give so many good gifts. Chief among them is the opportunity to lie down and wake up in peace. Please help us to be truly grateful for the many ways that the holy heritage of this nation has allowed us life, liberty, and the pursuit of unbounded happiness. And thank you for pouring out your many undeserved mercies upon us. Teach us to ever give heartfelt thanks. Amen.

THE JEWELRY INSURANCE INVENTORY FORM

What is your treasure?

1. Serving in the military requires sacrifice from veterans and those they leave at home. Ask God to place three military families on your heart. Pray for them and then do something practical to encourage them.

2. A Purple Heart may be given to someone who suffered for his nation. Jesus made the ultimate sacrifice when He gave His life for ours. Think about the sacrifices that have been made for us, and then thank God for those powerful examples of love.

3. Rewards are given to soldiers who serve well. As Christians, we're called to serve God faithfully. What are some traits that would help you better honor God?

4. Take the time right now to fervently pray for our country and its many brave veterans.

TWENTY-THREE

Heirloom Jewelry

Heirloom jewelry includes items with monetary or sentimental value that have been passed down from one generation to another. These can often include a mother's pearls, wedding rings from our grandmothers, or our grandfather's pocket watch. While some of the items of jewelry aren't valuable monetarily, all of the pieces are priceless from a sentimental standpoint as they bring back memories of loved ones who are no longer with us.

Sometimes the poorest man leaves
his children the richest inheritance.

—*Ruth E. Renkel*

FROM GENERATION TO GENERATION

After her mother passed away, Mary received several things that meant the world to her. One was her mother's jewelry box filled with both trinkets and valuable items. It was a box of cherished memories.

She pulled out a long strand of colorful beads. Her mother had allowed her to play with them when she was a little girl. Tears welled in her eyes as she remembered her mom's sweet voice saying, "Mary, you look beautiful. I want you to remember something for the rest of your life: You'll always be my princess. You are special to me and to God."

Mary pulled a set of cuff links from the jewelry box. They'd belonged to her daddy. She smiled as she remembered Sunday mornings from her childhood when she'd sat on the bed and helped her daddy place them in the cuffs of his white dress shirt before they left for church. She could close her eyes and almost hear his deep voice saying, "Mary-girl, always wear your best for Jesus."

Mary opened another drawer in the jewelry box, and there was her grandfather's pocket watch. Mary's daddy would sometimes let her hold it, but she wasn't allowed to play with it. He'd shared the history of the pocket watch with her, telling her it had been a gift from his great-grandfather, a present accompanied with these words: "Time is one of your most precious gifts. Spend it on God and your family."

She opened the hidden drawer in the jewelry box and

pulled out another special treasure—her mother's pearls. Mary's daddy had given them to her mother on their wedding day, a symbol of his love for her. Mary had worn them on her own wedding day, stroking their silky texture right before her daddy walked her down the aisle. He'd leaned over and kissed her just before they walked through the doors, and he'd said, "Put God first in your marriage, Mary-girl, and you and Bobby will be just fine."

Those pearls and that pocket watch were the most valuable things dollar-wise in her mother's jewelry box. Her parents had never had a lot of money. As Mary sorted through her mother's treasures that day, she realized that along with the contents of that jewelry box, they'd left her a far more valuable inheritance—they'd left her memories of faith, of love, and of loved ones who had walked with God and put Him first in their lives.

Someday Mary would get to share those stories and hand those heirloom pieces down to her own children. She loved the continuity of that—from generation to generation. But even more, she wanted to hand down the priceless gift of faith her parents had given her.

Dear God, help me to remember that the real treasures are the ones that come from you.

One generation shall praise thy works to another,
and shall declare thy mighty acts.
—*Psalm 145:4*

Father, it's easy to collect trinkets and baubles that don't really matter. Remind me of what is truly important and valuable. As I pass down heirloom items to my children and grandchildren, let them be sweet reminders of special times with a woman who loved them, a woman who wore her faith each day like a beautiful accessory. Help me to live my life in such a manner that future generations will look back and say, "She sure did love God." Amen.

THE JEWELRY INSURANCE INVENTORY FORM

What is your treasure?

1. What kind of family heirlooms do you have? What kind of spiritual heirlooms do you have? What are the spiritual heritage moments that stick out in your mind? Thank God for the people who have invested in you spiritually, and then give them a call or send them a note thanking them for the impact they've had on you.

2. Why are family heirlooms valuable to you? If it's sentimental value, what makes the item so special? Why are your spiritual heirlooms valuable to you? How have they touched or changed your life?

3. Have you ever squabbled with someone over material things? Was it worth it? How do you think God feels about that?

4. What we do now affects future generations. Spend some time in prayer for your family and ask God to give you a legacy of faithfulness.

TWENTY-FOUR

Love Letters

Whether coming from across town, across country, or from the other side of the world, love letters have inspired couples with the hope that, one day, the two might be finally and fully together. No matter which wartime conflict you're thinking of, a fighting man lived for mail call, holding firmly to the hope that his girl might have started a letter on its long journey toward him. No wonder they were so precious and were so frequently shared with others who weren't as lucky. Many couples married for years can still point to a precious pile of letters entwined with ribbon, with each studied word treated like purest gold.

Tender words scrawled by an adoring hand are
cherished forever by the much-loved heart.
—John Perrodin

DEAR DARLING

In the good old days, before there were e-mails, texts, instant messages, and multiple social media options for staying in touch, people actually took up a pen (or pencil) to write a letter. Yes, by hand! Real letters with thoughtful sentences, full paragraphs, and often, many pages of deep communication. They asked questions and expectantly waited for a response.

Some correspondence fit a special category known as "love letters." A love letter or note provided the chance for two people to tell each other their hopes and dreams. Only one rule applied to this kind of delightful free-for-all: patience. You sent your heart on paper and waited for the ever-faithful postal service to wing the reply back. These missives, long or short, were written in beautiful script on stationery or maybe scribbled on the back of a grocery list. Some people (yes, mostly men) even scrawled sweet nothings on napkins.

Women keep their treasures in jewelry boxes. Sentimental items such as love letters are just as valuable as expensive jewelry and are often tucked alongside gems for safekeeping. You probably have one or two—or many—of your own.

What fun it is to reread those words sent from the man who now passes grandchildren back and forth as you share a loveseat. Not so long ago he wrote you profound words that made your heart tingle. He spoke of all you meant to him and of how greatly he desired to make you his bride. These words still bring a tear or two today.

Yes, he's changed. Maybe you, too, have a few more

wrinkles or strands of gray than you once did. Still, the underlying words of love remain. Even if they aren't spoken as often as you'd like, you know that through actions and faithfulness, your devotion remains true. And it still melts your heart today when you find a sticky note with Xs and Os and vows of eternal affection on the bathroom mirror. That kind of gesture brings a smile as you make room in your jewelry box for another proclamation of love from your sweetheart.

God has also sent us some amazing love letters in His Word. Each book of the Bible can stand alone as a breathless narrative of the Creator reaching out to His children—and nothing is more precious than having the chance to read words of love from the One who holds our heart.

Jesus loved us so much that he gave His life for us. Did you get that? His *life*! Nothing could be more valuable than God's love. The key question is this: Do we look daily for the treasured reminders of His love that are sown throughout Scripture? Maybe it's time for us to pull out His love letter to us and take another long look.

◆ ◆

Forasmuch as ye are manifestly declared to be the
epistle of Christ ministered by us, written not with ink,
but with the Spirit of the living God; not in tables
of stone, but in fleshy tables of the heart.

—*2 Corinthians 3:3*

*Dear Father, I wish I understood more about you. I
really have no excuse. I know how to stay in touch
with those I care about. Today it's easier than ever.
But sometimes I make excuses when it comes to con-
necting with you, the King of my heart, my Lord and
the giver of life. All I have to do is crack open the
Bible to find exquisite letters of love and sacrifice,
hope and joy. Please help me to make my love relationship with my Savior even more powerful and real.
You are a love letter to the world, Lord. Make me one
as well. Open my eyes to the beauty of your message. Amen.*

THE JEWELRY INSURANCE INVENTORY FORM

What is your treasure?

1. Do you have a favorite love letter from your sweetheart? The Bible is God's love letter to us. What are some of your favorite Scriptures? Why are they precious to you? Look them up and spend some time thinking about them.

2. If we know that the Bible is God's love letter to us, why do we so often allow His Word to be a dust catcher on our bedside tables?

3. Write a love letter to God. Praise Him for all He's done for you, and then share that with others so that they can get a glimpse of your amazing God.

4. Sometimes the people who wrote us love letters leave us. That can break our hearts. God promises to *never* leave us. What does it mean to you to know that you can always count on God?

TWENTY-FIVE

Custom Jewelry

Custom jewelry is jewelry that is personalized for the user or buyer. It's usually one-of-a-kind, meaning that nobody else will have that exact piece of jewelry. This is sometimes done so colors will match an outfit, for a prospective bridegroom as he designs and purchases a unique engagement ring for his girlfriend, or to reflect the interests and personality of the wearer. Before starting the project, the craftsman has a plan for what the final product will become.

∽❧∾

You are a one-of-a-kind gem
in God's jewelry box.
—*Michelle Cox*

A Custom Design

Custom jewelry has been a recent trend, and many of us have special pieces like that in our jewelry boxes. Craft stores are filled with beads, baubles, and all the necessary pieces to make your own jewelry.

If you aren't crafty, someone can make it for you. Whenever I have trouble finding just the right jewelry for an outfit, I can take it to one of my friends and she will make the perfect necklace or earrings for me—and nobody else will have one just like it.

I recently learned about a company that makes custom bracelets. You can send in something in handwriting and have it engraved on the bracelet. That would be an awesome way to preserve something special from a loved one.

There are companies that sell charm bracelets, and women can select charms as remembrances of special moments. Other businesses sell necklaces that can be customized to reflect our individual interests.

But you know what? None of those pieces of jewelry happen without a plan. And the God who loves us so much that He's engraved our names on His hand has a purpose for each of us.

The jewelry maker doesn't just throw things together. Thought goes into each item. It's planned with care, with a vision for what the final piece will become.

It's the same with us spiritually. Before we were even born,

God—the master jeweler—had a purpose and a plan for each of us, and He knows what He wants the final result to be.

I can just imagine Him doing that with my friend Carol. She's a suburban homemaker who is the bling queen, but she frequently visits a men's prison, carrying the love of Jesus and the story of forgiveness to those who've never experienced that before. God designed her with a tender heart and a sunshine personality that draws people to her. She's one of God's custom jewels.

My friend Dee Dee is another of God's one-of-a-kind jewels. Even though she has experienced the loss of a child and serious health issues, she's a prayer warrior and an encourager who often delivers mason jars filled with homemade soup to friends who are going through hard times. When God designed Dee Dee, He gave her a caring heart, a sweet personality that comforts others, and a faith that can touch heaven with her prayers.

God had a unique plan for their lives, and He equipped them with all the skills they needed to accomplish those tasks.

Dear friend, just like Carol and Dee Dee, *you* are one of God's custom designs. He has a plan for *your* life that nobody else can fulfill. Are you using your talents for Him, or will they go to waste?

For I know the thoughts that I think toward you,
saith the LORD, thoughts of peace, and not of evil,
to give you an expected end.

—*Jeremiah 29:11*

Dear Lord, I don't want the gifts and talents you've given me to go to waste. Show me ways that I can glorify you by giving of myself. It humbles me to think that I'm one of your custom designs. How you have honored me. I don't want to let you down! Help me to fulfill the plan and purpose you have for my life. When I look at others, help me to see them as you see them. And when others look at me, help them to see you. Amen.

THE JEWELRY INSURANCE INVENTORY FORM

What is your treasure?

1. Just like God gave Carol and Dee Dee their unique ministries to men in prison and taking homemade soup to hurting friends, He has given *you* a unique set of gifts and talents. How are you using them for Him?

2. What gifts and talents do you have that are currently going unused? What do you think God will say when we stand before Him at the end of our lives with wasted talents?

3. Sometimes God's plans for us aren't the plans that we have ourselves. How does it affect us when we try to do our own thing instead of what He wants?

4. How can you use your gifts and talents to help someone else today? Ask God to bring three people to mind, and then follow through with whatever He places on your heart.

TWENTY-SIX

The Heart Necklace

Human hearts come in all shapes and sizes, just like people. And heart necklaces are often just as varied in size and the materials used to design them. A heart necklace speaks of love to a woman. Often given by her husband, child, or a dear companion, the heart necklace means "I love you, care about you, and think of you often." The giver wants the recipient to know she is a woman of immense value.

The best and most beautiful things
in the world cannot be seen or even touched. They
must be felt with the heart.

—Helen Keller

A Sign of Love

Sparkling and shining, your heart of gold hangs freely on an anchor link chain.

The heart shape is seen everywhere in jewelry pieces. They are formed from every conceivable metal, shell, stone, and wood. They come in every size. Some are adorned with diamonds or other gems. Others are old-fashioned with entwining filigree, or they're layered to give the heart depth and visual appeal.

The heart necklace is found everywhere because it's really the "happy face" of the jewelry industry. Who can argue with a heart? It makes you feel good and proclaims a certain message to the world. Namely, it says that you have someone special in your life. Maybe even the person who gave it to you.

The thought of a happy heart just makes us smile. It's the symbol of love, friendship, and all-around good times. Wearing a heart seems to say, "I am loved. Special. Look, all of you! Someone cares about me." Or you may have bought it for yourself (and there's nothing wrong with that) because you hope to one day meet the man who will capture your heart.

The jewelry you wear around your neck is silent. Maybe you are too at times. True feelings are hidden away when we dress and act as if there's nothing wrong. We think that if we look like we're in control, no one will know that we're scared and lonely and trembling inside. Hiding those feelings can impact us physically, emotionally, and even spiritually. If left

◇ ◇

untreated, a wounded heart can fester, releasing bitterness, anger, and fear into our lives.

But it's hard when our heart hurts. We want a loving relationship but have a less than perfect marriage. Or maybe a friend has shattered us with a lie or a child has broken our heart. Perhaps we are betrayed by a coworker who has promised to stand at our side, or a loved one has shared something that has rocked our faith. No matter how firm and strong we appear, a tender heart can be easily broken.

It is difficult to fully give over your heart. To do so takes the ultimate confidence in another. When you put yourself in someone else's hand, you risk disappointment, pain, and rejection. Thankfully, we know from Scripture that "the LORD is nigh unto them that are of a broken heart; and saveth such as be of a contrite spirit" (Psalm 34:18).

The next time you slip on your sweet sentimental jewelry, consider your own expectant heart. God gave you that solid, steady beat, and He can be trusted. Wholeheartedly.

◆ ◆

Delight thyself also in the LORD:
and he shall give thee the desires
of thine heart.
—*Psalm 37:4*

Dear Father, sometimes I act like I'm not worried or afraid, but you know the fear that is so often in my heart. On other days I pretend all is well with my world when my heart is really broken, shattered by circumstances. During those hard times, help me to remember that even my next breath is measured by you, and you are in control. Give me a heart for those I love. Help me to never stop caring, even when communication becomes difficult. I'm so grateful for the comfort you give me, for the times you've wrapped your arms around me and brought sweet peace. I love you, Lord. Amen.

THE JEWELRY INSURANCE INVENTORY FORM

What is your treasure?

1. Sometimes when we feel alone or sad, we try to hide our broken hearts from others. Why do we do that? God sees our hearts and He knows the truth. Spend some time with Him. Share your burdens and get a hug from heaven.

2. A heart necklace tells the world that we are loved. How can you tell the world (others) about how much God loves them? Ask Him to place three people on your heart.

3. Think about a time when someone hurt your heart. How did you respond to that situation? How do you think God wants you to react to situations like that?

4. What are some words of comfort that have helped to heal your heart? List some favorite Scriptures that have encouraged you in the past.

TWENTY-SEVEN

The Angel Pin

Angel pins can be made out of gold, silver, copper, or even ribbon or lace. They are often worn as a symbol of one's faith or as a reminder that God's guardian angels are watching over us. They can be a visible, tangible reminder that God is with us and taking care of us—surrounding us with His angels. And they make wonderful gifts to our friends and loved ones to remind them that we are praying for them and that God is always with them.

God does not comfort us to make us comfortable,
but to make us comforters.

—J. H. Jowett

Susan had finally gotten around to cleaning out her jewelry box. A special pin caught her eye. She didn't wear it often, but it was precious to her because of what it had meant during a difficult time in her life.

The long weeks at the hospital had taken their toll, leaving Susan physically and emotionally exhausted. Watching her mom, Betsy, go through months of cancer treatments had been heartbreaking. When she developed complications requiring hospitalization, it had been devastating for everyone.

Betsy had always been the comforter in the family, encouraging and praying for everyone and dispensing hugs that felt like they squeezed all the way to whatever ailed you. She'd always been a strong woman, gardening for hours at a time, cleaning until everything gleamed, and cooking wonderful feasts for family get-togethers.

Now she was so weak she couldn't even brush her hair. Her grandchildren had always been her joy, but she was too sick to even kiss them. Susan felt like her heart would break. The bad thing was that the one she normally went to for comfort was too sick to fill that role.

As the days went by in a seemingly never-ending fashion, the news from the doctors became progressively worse. Susan withdrew from everyone as she tried to numb the emotions that flooded her. She'd given until there was nothing left to give.

Susan's loved ones worried about her, but other than

prayer and meals for her family, nobody knew how to help her through this difficult time. But the next time Susan's friend Jennifer prayed for her, she added another request: *God, could you help me find some way to be a comfort to Susan?*

As she walked by the jewelry department at the department store the next day, an angel pin caught Jennifer's eye. It was as if God had whispered, *Take that to Susan.*

Jennifer purchased the angel pin and attached a note that said, *Always remember that God answers prayer and that His angels are watching over you.*

When Jennifer left the hospital after visiting Betsy and Susan, she quietly placed the box with the angel pin on the table where Susan would find it.

Tears flowed as Susan read Jennifer's note, and then that sweet comfort that only God can give flooded through her soul. The circumstances hadn't changed, but the reminder that God was in control made all the difference. That night when Susan hugged Betsy, she whispered, "Mama, His angels are watching over you."

A few days later, Betsy's health began to improve, all the way until the day she was pronounced cancer-free.

Are you going through a tough time? God *does* answer prayer. His angels *are* watching over you. As my pastor, Rev. Ralph Sexton, says, "Even when you can't track Him, you can trust Him."

◆ ◆

For he shall give his angels charge over thee,
to keep thee in all thy ways.
—*Psalm 91:11*

Dear Father, sometimes I'm overwhelmed by difficult situations. I'm so grateful to know you are always there during those times and that you do answer our prayers. I'm thankful that even when I don't understand the circumstances, you are still in control and are working out what's best for me. Just as Jennifer bought that angel pin to give comfort to Susan, help me to be an extension of your love and comfort to others who are facing difficult days. I love you, Lord. Thank you for being the ultimate comforter. Amen.

THE JEWELRY INSURANCE INVENTORY FORM

What is your treasure?

1. Susan's angel pin was a reminder of God's comfort during a tough time. Think of a time when God comforted you during difficult circumstances. How can you use what God did for you to help someone else?

2. Sometimes it's difficult to pray for ourselves when we're going through difficult times. Who do you know that's walking through tough days? Ask God to place three people on your heart. Pray for them and ask God how you can be a comfort to them.

3. Sometimes it's difficult when we don't understand *why* God is putting us through something hard. What do you need to do to trust Him during those times?

4. We often cry, complain, or even get mad at God when the pressures of life are especially tough. Why do you think He sends us through those times?

TWENTY-EIGHT

Gold Jewelry

G old jewelry is sought out by both collectors and criminals. That's because gold has intrinsic value as a precious metal. A story illustrates this point. Two robbers broke into a home. They weren't particularly bright, but they knew gold when they saw it. Or at least they thought they did. In a hurry, they grabbed the shiniest chains and bracelets from the ornate jewelry box. When the family returned, the dressing area was in shambles. Then the lady of the house started laughing. The criminals had taken only her brightest bling, not her best. Her gold-plated costume pieces were gone, but her most treasured pieces, though in plain sight, remained safely behind.

Real gold and real Christians
are both marked by their purity.
—*Michelle Cox*

WHAT LIES BENEATH?

It's easy to wrap a tawdry nickel necklace in a thin layer of gleaming gold to give it visual appeal. Gold-plated or filled jewelry isn't the same as genuine gold jewelry. Not by a long shot. In simplest terms, it's like taking a cheap metal locket or alloy rolo chain and dousing it with gold spray paint. The process of gold plating is more complex, but the result is the same. An item is disguised as something it's not.

Thankfully, certain signs can help us to discern the truth. Real gold is marked with a sign indicating the purity. Any jeweler will tell you such pieces may be stamped 12K or 12KT to mean "12-karat" gold. Honest craftsmen and distributors clearly tag their creations with GP or GF for "gold-plated" or "gold-filled" jewelry, respectively.

This allows us to purchase a piece that is designed to shine with the beauty of real gold while proclaiming that it's not. Still, some unwary buyers fail to look for such disclaimers and pay too much for something worth far too little.

Gold must be at least 10 karats to be considered genuine, and 24 is the maximum. Interestingly, 24-karat gold is too soft to fashion an entire chain. Ironically, then, if a sizeable piece of jewelry appears brilliant yellow like fine gold, it's probably not. Such gold may appear bright but the beauty is not to be believed. Another sure sign of a fake is discovered after time when the gold plating wears off and the core shows through. If it's real, it's real through and through.

Finally, there is the proverbial acid test that reveals the

actual content of any glittery golden metal. A sample of snake chain, for example, can be verified when scratched gently on a touchstone. Nitric acid is then daubed on the mark, and the chemical reaction tells the story. The stronger the acid required to dissolve the mark, the higher the quality of gold. There's no way to hide the truth. A fire assay, by contrast, will destroy your jewelry and leave behind only the purest particles of gold.

God similarly tests our hearts, warming us slowly in life's pressure cooker, burning away the impurities. During terrible trials when the veneer wears thin, do we dare look at what's below the surface? Are we made of God's glorious gold or something less precious? "And I will turn my hand upon thee, and purely purge away thy dross, and take away all thy tin" (Isaiah 1:25). May you know for sure, sooner rather than later.

The fear of the L<small>ORD</small> is clean, enduring for ever:
the judgments of the Lord are true and righteous
altogether. More to be desired are they than gold,
yea, than much fine gold: sweeter also than
honeycomb.

—*Psalm 19:9–10*

Lord, ever since the unblemished days in the garden, we've been confused about how to tell truth from lies. I know that in my own life there are times that I'm tricked into believing the unbelievable. Please grant me greater discernment so I can better serve you and others.

Also, help make my internal "mettle" like the purest gold, so that when you test me I will stand firm for you, not melt away in misery. In a world where so much is fake, people are looking for something real. Help me to be real for you so others will see Jesus in me. Burn away the impurities in my life so I can shine for you with the glowing light of your love. Amen.

◇ ◇

THE JEWELRY INSURANCE INVENTORY FORM

What is your treasure?

1. The thieves who broke into the home stole fake jewelry instead of the real gold. Have you ever gone after the wrong things and then realized God had something better for you? What did you learn from that?

2. Are you afraid of being robbed or other things? Fear can cripple us. Find five verses about forgetting fear and trusting in God. Write them down and then memorize them.

3. The thieves didn't have good discernment. They didn't know what was fake and what was real gold. What practical steps could help us strengthen our spiritual discernment?

4. Fragile gold plating can wear off of gold that isn't real to the core. Are you the real deal for God, or does your faith wear thin through the pressure of life? How can you be more durable as a Christian?

TWENTY-NINE

Religious Jewelry

Numerous jewelry items are available that express our religious beliefs. Necklaces with crosses, the passion nail, or the mustard seed are some examples. The prayer locket necklace includes a tiny box for placing one's special prayer requests, and there are charm bracelets that feature the Ten Commandments or Noah's ark. Religious-themed jewelry shares our faith in a visible way. When we wear this jewelry, we are giving a soundless testimony about what we believe and what is important to us.

The serene silent beauty of a holy life
is the most powerful influence in the world,
next to the might of God.

—*Blaise Pascal*

A Quiet Testimony

We've all seen women (and men) wearing religious jewelry, and most of us have at least one piece in our jewelry boxes. So why do people wear faith-themed jewelry? There are a variety of reasons—but they all have one thing in common: these pieces are a testimony of our faith and our love for God.

Think about some of the different pieces. The cross is an obvious one as it's a reminder of the sacrifice God made for all of us. Some crosses are ornate, some are simple, and still others have been crafted from two passion nails to represent the nails that pierced the hands and feet of Jesus as He gave His life on that rugged cross in place of ours.

A mustard seed necklace provides a reminder that it only takes a tiny bit of faith to move mountains. Most of us need frequent reminders about that, but can you imagine how much comfort that brings to someone facing a doctor's diagnosis of a terminal illness, or someone in the midst of a dire financial situation?

Small prayer box necklaces provide a secure place to put special prayer requests so folks can wear them around their necks, keeping those requests close to their hearts.

Purity rings are worn as reminders to young women to keep their hearts and bodies pure until their wedding night. I wonder how many girls have been in potentially compromising situations and looked down or felt that ring and escaped temptation. It's always a sweet part of a wedding when the bride swaps her purity ring for a wedding ring.

There are angel pins, necklaces, and bracelets—simple tokens to remind us that His angels are watching over us each and every day.

Other necklaces include silver boxes with the words *Holy Bible* on them or the Star of David. And sometimes there are inspiring messages or verses of Scripture on them, such as, "I can do all things through Christ which strengtheneth me" (Philippians 4:13).

No matter what piece of religious jewelry we put on, we need to remember we're giving a message when we wear it. We're making a statement that says, *This is what I believe.*

And that's an important reminder for all of us when we sport those pieces of jewelry—others are watching to see how we really live. It might be years down the road, but somewhere along the way, I can promise you someone will say, "I've been watching you to see how you lived for God." Are we good representatives of Him, or does our jewelry say one thing and our lives and testimonies say something else?

Wear your faith, and wear it well.

That the communication of thy faith may become effectual by the acknowledging of every good thing which is in you in Christ Jesus.

—*Philemon 1:6*

Father, just as we wear our religious jewelry as a silent testimony to others, I want my life to show my abundant love for you. Let my words match my actions. Keep me pure and clean. Help me to be a good example for you. Remind me that others are watching, and that the way I live each day can lead them to you or turn them away from you. Help me to be faithful. Help me to bring honor to your name every day in every way. Amen.

THE JEWELRY INSURANCE INVENTORY FORM

What is your treasure?

1. Why do you think we forget the simple message of the mustard seed? Have you ever had that kind of faith? Tell about some of the moments of faith you've had and what God did for you in those times.

2. Why is the cross important to you? What can you do to help share the message of God's love and sacrifice with others?

3. A prayer box necklace allows one to place a special prayer request inside. What special prayers have you prayed, and how has God answered them?

4. Have you ever thought about buying a piece of faith-based jewelry to give to a friend who is going through a difficult time? How could you use that gift as a springboard to encourage your friend or to talk to an unsaved friend about God?

THIRTY

The Jewelry Box

A jewelry box is a container for women to store what is precious to them—their jewelry, keepsakes, love letters, and so on. Jewelry boxes come in a variety of sizes and shapes, but there are some important considerations when buying one of them. You'll need to decide if you want a jewelry box for a child or an adult. Wood is best because it helps to control the moisture, which keeps jewelry from tarnishing. And you'll want to make sure there is a soft, nonabrasive lining, especially for your pearls and gems.

Just like a jewelry box, what's on
the inside of each of us is far more valuable
than what is on the outside.
—Michelle Cox

◆ ◆

WHAT'S YOUR TREASURE?

When our family goes on vacation to Hilton Head Island, one of the things my daughters-in-law and I like to do together is to go to the consignment stores. Because it's an upscale area, we often find awesome treasures.

On one of those trips, my daughter-in-law Laurel was thrilled to find a like-new jewelry box. Now this wasn't your standard jewelry box. This was a large one with a variety of lined drawers that opened out to the side and with pull-out doors for hanging her necklaces.

Laurel has a lot of jewelry, and this jewelry box was perfect for organizing her earrings, rings, and bracelets, and for keeping her necklaces from getting tangled. She bought the jewelry box for a fraction of what she would have paid for it if she'd bought it brand-new.

Laurel's jewelry box is awesome, but I discovered another jewelry box recently that I think is so smart. The designers took one of those freestanding full-length mirrors and created a box behind it to make a jewelry armoire. It has hooks for hanging necklaces, cushioned areas for rings, and compartments for earrings and bracelets. And then the mirror is right there for you to see how each item will look.

Sweet friends, we need to take just as much care with our hearts as we do with our jewelry boxes. Just as my daughter-in-law bought her jewelry box, God paid the price for us. Did you get that? He looked at us and saw something valuable, someone He could use. We're not God's discarded jewelry;

◇ ◇

we're His priceless gems. Like glancing at a mirrored jewelry armoire—we need to take a look into His mirror of grace so we'll see the valuable jewels He made in us.

So why are we living as if we're costume jewelry when we're one of His precious gems? We need to get rid of the junk in our lives, untangling the jumbled messes we've made. Just like the nonabrasive lining in our jewelry boxes, we need to line our hearts with His Word, locking out things that would be harmful for us and polishing our hearts with prayer so that no tarnish is found there. And, then, just as we display our jewelry boxes in a special place, God can put us on display for others who need to see Him.

That brings us to some important questions: What's *your* treasure? Are you spending your time and money on things that don't count, or are you accumulating treasures that will matter for eternity?

What priceless items will you place in your spiritual jewelry box?

For where your treasure is,
there will your heart be also.

—*Matthew 6:21*

Dear Father, a jewelry box sits on a shelf or dresser and does nothing but gather dust. I don't want to be like that. I want to be used by you whenever and wherever I can. Help me to read your Word, to listen to you, and to spend time talking with you each day. Take the tangled messes in my life and untangle them with your love and mercy. Help me to put things of value in my heart, not useless junk. Make me a gleaming jewel for you so that when others see me, they see a shining reflection of you. Amen.

THE JEWELRY INSURANCE INVENTORY FORM

What is your treasure?

1. Is your jewelry box cluttered with junk jewelry? In much the same way, we clutter our hearts with junk that shouldn't be there. What do you need to remove from your heart and life so that you can sparkle for Him?

2. Jewelry boxes are useful to their owners. What are you doing to be of value to God? Are you using the talents He's given you?

3. What are you putting into your jewelry box? What are you putting into your heart? Are you talking to God? Are you spending time in His Word? Are you having a daily quiet time to listen to Him?

4. Women spend a lot of time on their hair and makeup and on picking out their clothes and jewelry. Are you putting as much effort into becoming a woman of beauty on the inside?

Isn't it amazing how you can find glimpses
of God on every item in your jewelry box?
As you put on your jewelry each day,
remember something important:
God considers *you* one of His jewels—
a woman of infinite value.
Now go out and sparkle for Him.

We would love to hear how these devotionals have touched and impacted your life. Please contact Michelle and John to share your thoughts and stories with us.

We promise to write back.

Acknowledgments

Many people are involved in making a book become a reality, and we'd like to express our gratitude to them. Thanks so much to Carlton Garborg for catching the vision for *God Glimpses from the Jewelry Box* with us, and to David Sluka, Michelle Winger, Bill Watkins, Darcie Clemen, and the rest of the team at BroadStreet Publishing Group. It's been a joy working with you.

Thank you to Margaret Skiles and our beta readers who took the time to read our manuscript and came back with valuable suggestions and comments. You helped make our book better.

There are no words to express our gratitude for our prayer team. You are the wind beneath our words, and we couldn't do what we do without you. We appreciate your prayers, your encouragement, and your willingness to pray for us and our work.

I (Michelle) would like to thank my coauthor, John Perrodin, for being the best coauthor in the world. Seriously. You bring so much to our projects and make the experience enjoyable from start to finish.

I'd also like to thank my husband, Paul, for being my biggest cheerleader, praying for me, being my sounding board for ideas, and helping out around the house so that I can have time to write. I love you, baby, and you're an important part of all that I do.

I (John) have been doubly blessed by having an amazing coauthor, Michelle Cox, who not only works harder than any writer I know, but also has believed in our God Glimpses concept for years. Literally. Thank you, Michelle! Your faithful fortitude and hopeful attitude have truly made this book a reality.

I would also like to express my heartfelt gratitude to my wife, Sue. What an adventure we've shared—and what a precious gift our time together is. I need you and love you—and always will. Through you I have seen many a powerful glimpse of God's love. Thanks, sweetie.

Most importantly, we'd like to thank God for the idea for this book, for answering our prayers and sending inspiration as we started each chapter, and for allowing us to write for Him.

Finally, thanks so much to all of you—our readers. We prayed for you as we worked on *God Glimpses from the Jewelry Box*. We hope that the words will touch your hearts and provide glimpses of Him and that you'll realize you truly are one of God's priceless jewels. Thank you for coming on this adventure in the jewelry box with us.

About the Authors

MICHELLE COX

Known for her "encouragement with a Southern drawl," Michelle Cox is a speaker and an award-winning, best-selling author. She is a member of the blog team for *Guideposts*. Her "Life with a Southern Grandmother" column runs twice each week at www.Guideposts.org.

Michelle is a contributing writer for *Leading Hearts Magazine* and does reviews and interviews for ChristianCinema. com. She has written for FoxNews.com, Focus on the Family, *WHOA Magazine for Women,* and a variety of other publications and sites. Michelle has been a guest on numerous television and radio programs, including *Hannity* and *Focus on the Family*.

She is the creator of the Just 18 Summers® brand of parenting products and resources. Visit her at www.just18summers. com, on Twitter @michelleinspire, and on Facebook at www. Facebook.com/MichelleCoxInspirations and www.Facebook. com/just18summers.

JOHN PERRODIN

Since childhood, John has loved books and wanted to be a writer. A registered nurse, he works as a patient representative for Centura Health Services.

John coauthored *Simple Little Words* with Michelle Cox and the Renegade Spirit trilogy novels with Jerry B. Jenkins. An attorney, speaker, and journalist, he wrote *3-Minute Devotions for Grads* and contributed to various devotional volumes, including *The Spirit Calling*. He has also prepared Bible commentaries, written magazine articles, and personally mentored authors who want to improve their skills.

John has worked for Focus on the Family, Promise Keepers, Alliance Defending Freedom, the Jerry Jenkins Writers Guild, and Alive Literary Agency. He lives with his fantastic wife and remarkable children in Colorado.

More God Glimpses

GOD GLIMPSES FROM THE TOOLBOX
USING TOOLS TO BUILD MEN OF CHARACTER

What's in your toolbox? Most of us have hammers and screwdrivers for repairs, and of course power tools—because nothing brings greater happiness than making a mess and generating a lot of noise.

But did you know that God's fingerprints can be found in our toolboxes as well? We can uncover amazing spiritual lessons tucked between our pliers and wrenches. Sometimes we act as if God is distant, but God glimpses are present in every aspect of our lives. We just have to look for them.

Take a trip through thirty items in a toolbox and discover encouragement, inspiration, and confirmation that God is so close you can reach out and touch Him. Get powered up to live as a man of character and strength.

INTRODUCTION

WHAT'S IN YOUR TOOLBOX?

Guys, what's in your toolboxes? Most of us have hammers and screwdrivers for home repairs. Tools for demo work. And power tools—because nothing brings greater happiness than making messes and generating *lots* of noise.

We'll admit that sometimes we don't use the best judgment when we do things. Proof of that can be found in blackened nails where we've hit our thumbs instead of the boards, bruises we wear as badges of honor, and cuts we've received from sharp pieces of metal. Yes, we keep the bandage folks in business!

When we look into our toolboxes, it's easy to see the items that are in there. But what most of us haven't discovered before are the amazing spiritual lessons hiding between the pliers and the wrenches.

Glimpses of God are present in every aspect of our lives if we'll just open our eyes and look around. That's the premise for the *God Glimpses* book series: to take important spiritual truths and apply them to ordinary experiences, such as the items found in a toolbox or jewelry box, a visit to the gym, or a day in the garden. We *can* discover God's will and purpose for our lives if we'll just take time to catch a glimpse of Him.

God often mentions tools and building in the Bible. Jesus spent His childhood with His earthly father as Joseph shared his knowledge of carpentry and building skills. Men used tools to construct the cross and then drove nails into the hands and feet of our Savior as He hung on that rugged tree. How appropriate then, that *God Glimpses from the Toolbox: Using Tools to Build Men of Character* is an inspirational book for men featuring the tools found in a toolbox.

Each of the chapters includes a definition of a tool and the spiritual application gleaned from it. Then, inspirational stories feature an anecdote about building, followed by a quote, a prayer, and a verse of Scripture that hammers home the truths of each chapter. A "building permit" page (asking, "What will I permit God to do in *my* life?") provides thought-provoking questions at the end of each chapter.

Guys, we don't know about you, but we want to be powered up and ready for God to use our lives. We want to be dependable tools in His toolbox. Please join us as we look for God glimpses from the toolbox.